SWASHBUCKLING SOCIAL STUDIES:

DRAMA ACTIVITIES AND CREATIVE WRITING TO MAKE SOCIAL STUDIES COME ALIVE

Text set in Dante and Brandon Grotesque.
Cover design by Cover Me Darling
Book design by Inkstain Design Studio
Printed in the United States of America.

ISBN-13: 978-0692879733
ISBN-10: 0692879730

Volume one: American History

SWASHBUCKLING SOCIAL STUDIES:
DRAMA ACTIVITIES AND CREATIVE WRITING TO MAKE SOCIAL STUDIES COME ALIVE

Dr. Sarah Philpott
Dr. Thomas N. Turner
Dr. Jeremiah Clabough

PRAISE

"Swashbuckling Social Studies infuses creative writing in the content area and does so in an engaging, creative, and fun way. Move over worksheet – there is a new purpose and style of writing that is surely poised to transform the social studies classroom!" —Timothy Lintner, Ph.D., Assistant Vice Chancellor for Academic Affairs, Professor, University of South Carolina Aiken

"This teacher activity book makes learning social studies exciting for students! The activities are excellent for an array of learning styles. They include hands-on learning that brings critical thinking and creativity together in a manner allowing students to learn how to synthesize information at a deeper level." —Kenneth Carano, Ph.D., Associate Professor, Western Oregon University; Co-Coordinator, Center for Geography Education in Oregon; and Executive Editor, *Oregon Journal of the Social Studies*

"Swashbuckling Social Studies is taking age-old topics from history and modernizing them into something every child can relate to and enjoy. Students are literally taking subjects of the past and bringing them to life again in the 21st century! And, just like Common Core, Swashbuckling is revolutionizing the way we think about assessing students for understanding. These creative activities challenge students to use expressive language and dialogue in non-traditional writing formats to demonstrate true mastery of the material. Furthermore, the activities in this book are a great way to differentiate for kids who may struggle with text that is usually written in a rigid, non-fiction format." —Kerri Lawson, Reading Coach and Award-Winning Educator

"The C3 Framework by the National Council for the Social Studies (NCSS) Dimension 4, Communicating Conclusions states individually and with others, students use writing, visualizing, and speaking to communicate conclusions. As a retired elementary social studies teacher, former adjunct professor of elemen-

tary social studies methods, and NCSS Elementary Social Studies Teacher of the Year 2001, the goal of any elementary social studies teacher is to have students engage in social studies content, historical facts and figures through drama activities and creative writing. Swashbuckling Social Studies gives a plethora of ways to develop creative drama and writing with a rubric for each." —Dwight Herold, Ed.D., Past President, Iowa Council for the Social Studies

"Drama and creative writing not only teach critical thinking skills and shape a young student's development in and of themselves, but also when they are integrated into classroom curriculums, they also create a dynamic learning experience. Swashbuckling Social Studies is a well-researched program that uses drama and creative writing to bring social studies to life. The activities will engage young students and the methodology is clearly laid out for teachers to build on the many samples included." —Lauren Brown Shepherd, Executive Director of Athens Area Council for the Arts

"As a homeschooling mom, I understand how important it is for children to love learning; as a professional actor, dancer, and theatre teacher, I appreciate the role arts play for the mental, intellectual, social, and emotional development of students. With a program like Swashbuckling Social Studies, the teacher can introduce important points in history in such a way that will click with even the most reluctant student. Using the arts to teach - what a way to learn!" —Kelly Balch Borwick, Home School Mom to three and Professional Actor and Theatre Teacher

PREFACE

Swashbuckling Social Studies: Drama Activities and Creative Writing to make Social Studies Come Alive encourages young scholars to channel their passions into social studies, reading, writing, researching, public speaking, and dramatic activities!

Students are thrilled to take center stage in the classroom as they perform short monologues, songs, skits, and learn to write their own theatrical pieces. Teachers are delighted to see students learn and research social studies content.

Imagine King George III rapping about the American Revolution, Jane Addams and President Benjamin Harrison texting about the Hull House, and Paul Revere whining about his midnight ride. *Swashbuckling Social Studies* is jam-packed with creative writing and drama projects.

Not only does this resource provide sample monologues and skits for students to perform and directions for students to pen their own scripts, it allows young scholars to put words into the mouths of social studies topics which adds excitement and humor to content learning.

WHAT RESEARCH SAYS ABOUT WRITING

The form of playwriting presented in this book helps students to sort through research and construct their findings and impressions into a novel writing creation. Students need ample opportunities, such as the ones presented in this text, to simply write.

The National Commission on Writing (2003) said, "If students are to make knowledge their own, they must struggle with the details, wrestle with the facts and rework raw information and dimly understood concepts into language they can communicate to someone else. In short, if students are to learn, they must write."

WHAT RESEARCH SAYS ABOUT DRAMA

Using the dramatic arts is another manner in which students learn content (Burstein & Knotts, 2010). This emotional way of connecting students to content through the use of drama can help students remember historical facts and concepts (Turner, 2004). It also adds excitement in the classroom, helps students understand various perspectives of individuals involved in history and helps students understand historical events because it adds "depth and dimension to the plot, setting, and characters" (Kornfeld & Leyden, 2005, p. 230).

In addition to adding excitement and passion towards content in the classroom, drama helps student understand various perspectives of individuals involved in history, as well as historical events because it adds "depth and dimension to the plot, setting, and characters" (Kornfeld and Leyden, 2005, p. 230). Drama also helps students better comprehend textbooks and other content-area media (Rosler, 2008).

USING CREATIVE WRITING + DRAMA IN THE CLASSROOM

Drama and creative writing are the perfect pedagogy companions. Making use of the projects in this book gives students the opportunity to write, communicate information with others, and therefore internalize content knowledge.

The creative writing activities included in *Swashbuckling Social Studies* can be adapted for almost any social studies lesson. By using these projects, teachers motivate students to investigate social studies and present information in a novel format. While students may retain information by writing a traditional biographical report about the life of Abraham Lincoln, they might be more motivated to use historical information if given them the opportunity to create a rap song about his life!

The intent of this teacher-friendly resource is for educators to have a variety of creative social studies writing projects at their disposal so that students can learn through the process of writing. Students will have so much fun writing that they won't realize they are actively engaged in the research skills of struggling with details and wrestling with facts. In the end, they will communicate facts and information in a fresh format.

All of the writing activities can be turned into dramatic pieces for students to perform in the classroom. Not only does this book provide pre-written monologues that can be used in the classroom but also provides students the opportunity to become playwrights.

What happens to all those wonderful (*well, usually wonderful!*) student-composed writings? Typically, the cycle goes like this:

Student labors over writing. Student turns in writing. Writing goes into the teacher's bag. Teacher grades the writing at home. Teacher returns the writing with a grade and comments. Writing goes into student's backpack. Writing may or may not be read by anyone else.

Swashbuckling Social Studies allows teachers the opportunity to break this cycle by providing students a vehicle for sharing their own work. Authors can perform their own works individually or an "acting troupe" can perform the works of reluctant actors or great writers in the classroom. Not only are students learning social studies content through writing their own pieces, but they will also be learning content by watching the performances of other students.

You don't have to be an experienced director to help your students use drama in the classroom. All you need to do is model how students can read their pieces "in character," provide a safe environment for students to express themselves, and then give willing (and reluctant) students the opportunity to perform.

To ease into performance-mode, have students chorally read the pieces aloud all at once. This quick drama activity builds fluency and gives all students an opportunity to perform. Later you might extend opportunities for individuals to perform pieces during class-time. These drama pieces are a great learning activity for the start or end of class.

How you utilize these resources is up to you. Just be aware that your students might have so much fun that they forget learning is taking place!

HOW TO USE THIS BOOK

Each creative writing activity in *Swashbuckling Social Studies* includes samples and a step-by-step instruction sheet so students can easily follow the directions to pen their own writings. Also included is a sample rubric for assessing student writing.

Here is an example of how to utilize the writing projects in your classroom.

Teach the content and explain the project you would like completed. Be excited about the project—your enthusiasm goes a long way!

Show a sample or model the completed project so students can establish a schema of what they are aiming to create.

Provide a copy of the directions checklist and go over the guidelines. Make sure to articulate any additional instructions.

Explain how the work will be assessed. For example, provide a rubric ahead of time so students can be sure to meet your expectations.

Allow adequate time, resources, and independence to complete the project.

Afford time to share completed project with classmates. Let the budding actors and actresses perform their works.

Be prepared to see amazing work from your students!

CONTENTS

WHINES

"Will you please stop complaining?"

Grumbling and moaning is the nature of the "social studies *whine*." A whine is a form of writing that students can read aloud, react to, and write themselves as a form of reporting as they capture the essence of an individual, place, or thing. Add in a little humor or interest and you've got a winning piece of writing.

Ideas for Using Whines in the Classroom:

Whine-Off: Students in the classroom read their written whines aloud for all to hear. Decide who is the whiniest.

Choral Read: All students in the classroom read a whine aloud together. Everyone has fun and builds fluency while acting out the whines. Discuss why the subject is whining.

Anticipatory Set: Perform a whine at the beginning of a unit to build excitement about the subject. For example, start a unit about the American Revolution with a whine from Paul Revere.

Quick Assessment: Call on a student at the end of a lesson to perform an ad-lib whine. See if the student includes main content points.

Vivid Viewpoints: Discuss with students the different viewpoints that the whiners presented.

WRITING WHINES

Woe is me!

Choose a historical figure, geographical location, event, or inanimate historical object and write a whine that the topic might be guilty of saying. Use the blanks provided to pen some ideas you have before you write your final project.

STEPS TO TAKE:

1. Choose a historical figure, geographic location, event, or inanimate historical object (i.e. building, artifact, or monument).

Topic Ideas:

2. Search for facts about the topic and imagine why they might whine.

A Few Facts to Include:

3. Don't complain, but use the above facts to creatively write a few whiney paragraphs. Write like you imagine the character you would talk. Use words they might utter and be persuasively whiney.

The Whine of Paul Revere

Revere's the name, Paul Revere, and you should know that I *really* don't like poets.

More specifically, I detest that rhyming hack, Hank Longfellow. If you read what that old scribbler said, you'd think that all I did for the Revolution, that all I did during my *life*, in fact, was throw myself on a horse and ride through the countryside shouting, "The British are coming!"

And thank you very much, Longfellow was incorrect on a couple of counts.

I had to walk a lot, actually, after those regulars confiscated my horse. But, I want you and Hank to know that I was more than a messenger boy.

I was the best man in the silver game from Boston to New York and back.

I was aces in the etching biz, too.

But even more important than that, I was the top lithographer in the colonies. I printed pictures that swung public opinion. Changed history in fact. I turned harassment and riot by a bunch of ne'er do wells into an acts of heroic and patriotic martyrdom. Got that?

I created the Boston Massacre almost single-handed. I modestly say that I might have even given the Revolution a cause.

And I did it all on my own too.

I didn't have much time to go to school. I was the big kid, the oldest boy. You know the drill. In my day that meant I learned dad's trade and went to work. Since my dad was a gold and silversmith, that's what I became.

Before I was out of knee britches, I had my own business.

Okay, so even grown men wore knee britches back then. But I did start young.

Before you knew it I was up to my silver smithin' neck in politics…big time. I don't like to brag, but I was the main chief in that little "Indian Raid" they now call the Boston Tea Party. I looked real good in war paint and feathers. So there! I tossed tea crates into the harbor like I was trying to turn the Atlantic into a teapot.

Your quill-boy Longfellow forgot that, didn't he?

I was the "top son" in the Son's of Liberty, too. I became what we called a "North End mechanic." Pretty cool name, huh? Well, we "mechanics" patrolled the streets to watch the movements of the British troops and Tories. You might call us the first American street gang.

Me and my homeboys were getting ready for a revolution. We decided we needed a syndicate, so I rode up to Portsmouth. I gathered some of those New Hampshire boys and had them raid the Regulars military stores. Then, I set them up to attack Fort William and Mary. That practically started the American Revolution in itself. But no one ever talks about that.

Okay, okay! So I did ride the horse, I did wake up a lot of the militia, and I did warn the minutemen to grab their guns. But I NEVER once shouted, "The British are coming!"

That would have been stupid.

We all considered ourselves British. What I yelled was "The *Regulars* are coming!" You might think that writers like Longfellow the poet would have at least done the research.

The Whine of Benedict Arnold

You know what I think? History is totally unfair, is what I think!

I mean UNFAIR!

Why, for four years I was a war hero, for goodness sakes! I was the idol of my troops! They loved me! I was the hero of the Battle of Saratoga! Everyone knows that!

I won that battle, totally uncaring for my own life. Horses were shot out from underneath me—rallying the troops, the whole thing. And everyone knew that Gates, that armchair general, should never have gotten all the credit.

I can tell you that the only horse he was ever going to get on was headed AWAY from the battle, not toward the fight. And could we look at the invasion of Quebec? Sure the whole thing failed. But who saved the army? I did, of course!

And the troops loved me for it. I was their hero.

But does history make much of that? No, it does not! All history cares about are a few plans about a fort that *just happened* to get in the hands of a British officer who was *just dumb* enough to get caught.

Now if history had a wife who was anything like my wife, then history would understand all right! I tell you that woman of mine was always nagging. "You don't get paid enough", she'd say.

And then she'd throw in "my cousin, who is only captain in the British army gets TWICE as much money, and it's REAL money!"

And then she'd tell me that she never had anything to wear, and that the British were going to win the war anyway, and I'd just get myself hanged!

What man could live with that day in and day out?

But does history think of that? Oh, no! All it does is make my name synonymous with *traitor*. If history had been married, it would probably understand, but since it isn't, General Grant keeps all the credit for himself.

The Whine of the Wild West

It's not fair. The Wild West gets no respect. We brought America a bunch of varmints, horse thieves, scoundrels, bushwhackers, and yellow bellied cowards…the stuff that all good television westerns are made of!

But still, we get no respect.

People just want to go on and on about the American Revolution or the U.S. Civil War, but the most interestin' time in American history is the Wild West.

Most people reckon the Wild West started as Americans began to push past the Mississippi River in search of good land. This spirit of American exploration led to new states such as Texas, New Mexico, and California, to name just a few. Folks never mention this though. After the U.S. Civil War, people want to take a nap until the beginning of the 20th century.

The Wild West is more captivatin' than either the American Revolution or the U.S. Civil War. Several happenins' in the Wild West are still talked about today, such as the Alamo, Battle at the OK Corral, Battle of Little Big Horn, and California Gold Rush. The time of the Wild West provided several new items such as barbwire and steel plow. All of this stuff had a big imprint on U.S. history! Why I'd say the invention of barbwire is better than a good ol' pan of cornbread and beans since it let us keep all the cows in one area instead of us chasing them all the time.

The Wild West also brought us the cowboy to provide law and order in a lawless frontier. Many legendary characters of the Wild West include Billy the Kid, Doc Holiday, and Jesse James. There were several Hollywood actors that brought this mythical time period alive including John Wayne and Clint Eastwood. The Wild West created the Western TV and movie genre filled with shootouts and ornery outlaws. All of this is because of the events in the Wild West, and yet, no respect. You're dang-blasted welcome, America!

The Whine of Wild Bill Hickok

Wyatt Earp was a tin horn.

Bat Masterson was a pencil pusher.

Pat Garrett was a bad friend.

If you want to talk about a *real* lawman of the Old West, it has to be me—Wild Bill Hickok. I looked the part with my cross gun belts and twin colts. I'm the luckiest son of a gun around. I even acted the part. But who do they make movies about? Earp! Garett! Even Masterson! I've never gotten my share of the credit.

I tell you, it just ain't fair. It's slanderous!

Those town newspapers and dime novels always get their facts wrong. Half the time, I ended up looking like the bad guy. But look here! I've been a stage coach driver, a scout for the army, a guide, AND an officer of the law. And above all, I was not a man anyone wanted to fool with.

Why, when that newspaper in Tombstone said I had an utter disregard for human life, what could I say? Can I help it if the six shooter is the "law of the land"?

I mean when someone throws down on me, I am going to kill him, not give him another chance. What would you do?

Why I don't know myself how I get into so many darn "sitch-ee-ations," but when I do, well things are going to happen. Every man I ever killed was in self-defense.

Well, that, or in the performance of my official duty.

Like last month, I was in a saloon. .strictly in the line of duty, mind you. Two mean lookin' hombres armed to the teeth entered by opposite doors. I sized up the predicament in half a second and realized I had to draw both my pistols.

With one quick move I shot the one guy in front of me, and at the same time, I plugged the other man behind me with my other six shooter resting on my shoulder.

Used the mirror over the front door, I did. Now that's what I call shootin'!

Call it luck if you want, but it was skill, I say.

But did I get credit, praise, or even support?

I did not!

Instead, all I heard for weeks was cries of, "police brutality!"

I tell you, it's hard being a living legend when your name isn't Earp or Masterson. But now that I am up here in Wyoming, breathing in this cool air, I think I'll relax and play a little poker.

I'm feelin' lucky.

The Whine of Pike's Peak

I say it categorically. I AM a peak.

Not a great peak, mind you. I can live with that, BUT, I *am* a peak. At 14,110 feet tall I am called "America's Mountain," so I deserve respect. Unfortunately, I really don't get any.

Maybe it's because I am *only* the thirty-first highest peak in Colorado.

Not the first.

Not the second.

Not even in the top ten…but the thirty-first. Sigh.

Who wants to buy a t-shirt that says "I climbed the thirty-first highest peak in the state?"

But even my awesome name, "America's Mountain," doesn't garner respect. Other Colorado mountains have cool names like Mount Massive, or are named after presidents like Mount Lincoln and Mount Wilson.

Me? I'm named after a man named Zebulon Pike, a loser if there ever was one.

Seriously, who has ever heard of Zebulon Pike?

Why, even historians call him the "Lost Pathfinder." The only things Zeb Pike ever did was lead an expedition into the Southwest, without the President's authority or knowledge, mind you.

The only other thing of note about ol' Zeb was that he let a mine get the better of him in the War of 1812. Poor Zeb. Rest in peace. But here is what makes being named after him even worse—Old Zeb never climbed me, never named me, and probably never even *saw* me.

Sheesh!

That's just the start of it. You wouldn't believe how many losers seem to latch on to me. Literally. In the 1850s, gold-searching miners painted signs on their wagons that said, "Pike's Peak or Bust!"

What happened to most of them? You guessed it; they went BUST!

Then, there was this lady, the very first woman to climb me—Mrs. Julia Archibald Holmes.

No problem there. I made her a famous woman, right?

I wish!

What is she famous for?

The type of underwear she wore while climbing me. They call her the "Bloomer Girl." It's downright embarrassing.

Oh, yeah, so you want to know why they call me "America's Mountain"? It's nothing more than tourist hype. In 1885, they built a carriage road to my summit. Then, in 1901, a two-cylinder car called a "locomobile" made it to my top.

And the final insult happened in 1915 when they got the big idea to build a motor road up to me and then held a road race.

I was mortified! A road? I ask you—what self-respecting peak has a road going up it and cars racing to the top? You're supposed to climb a peak with ice axes, crampons, ropes, blood, sweat, tears, and all that stuff. You are not supposed to climb a peak by simply driving up a road!

America's Mountain? More like America's Minin' Bloomer Highway!

BRAGS

"What a braggart!"

Boasting is the nature of the social studies brag. Brags are forms of writing that students can read aloud, react to, and write themselves as a form of reporting. They try to capture the essence of an individual, place, or thing in a boastful manner. Add in a little humor or interest and you've got a winning piece of writing.

Ideas for Using Brags in the Classroom:

Brag-Off: Students in the classroom read their written brags aloud for all to hear. Decide whose is the most pompous.

Choral Read: All students in the classroom read a brag aloud. Everyone has fun and builds fluency while acting out the brag. Discuss why the subject is bragging.

Anticipatory Set: Perform brags at the beginning of a unit to build excitement about the subject. For example, start a unit about geography with a brag from Pike's Peak.

Quick Assessment: Call on student at the end of a lesson to perform an ad-lib brag. See if the student includes some of the main content points.

Vivid Viewpoints: After student performances, compare and contrast various viewpoints that were presented.

WRITING BRAGS

How sweet am I?

Choose a historical figure, geographical location, event, or inanimate historical object and write a brag they might tell about themselves. Imagine that they are their greatest cheerleader. Use the blanks provided to pen some ideas you might have before your write your final project.

STEPS TO TAKE:

1. Choose a historical figure, geographic location, event, or inanimate historical object (i.e. building, artifact, or vehicle).

Topic ideas:

2. Find facts about the topic. What might he, she, or it brag about?

Brag ideas:

3. Use facts to creatively write a few vain paragraphs. Write like you imagine the character you chose would talk. Think about the perspective you are taking when writing the brag. Are you writing as the subject's mother, the subject's enemy, the subject himself, the subject's jealous assistant, or someone else?

A few facts to include:

The Brag of Christopher Columbus

My name is Christopher Columbus, but you can call me Chris.

I'm far too modest to tell you that I am the best seaman to ever have sailed the seven seas and the smartest to boot. The King of Spain even called me, "Admiral of the Ocean Seas." Pretty sweet title, huh?

I'm much too modest to tell most people that information.

I had this theory that the world was round, and that you could get to India and all its riches by sailing west. Well, to tell you the truth, it wasn't really my theory, but I was the only one to give it a shot and test it out.

Until I came along, there were only two ways to get to India or China: you could either kill yourself by going through extreme conditions of the short path—deserts that would burn you up and mountains that would freeze you to death (plus this route ran you into every robber, thief, and killer that ever rode a camel or a mountain pony). Or, you could take the long path, and I do mean *long*, and travel by ship all the way around Africa. On that route you'd run into every killer-diller storm and every nasty ruthless pirate the sea had to offer. Either of these ways had king-sized dangers, but I knew there had to be an easier way.

All you had to do was sail straight west and you'd run right into India.

The problem was that I couldn't get anyone to believe it. The Italians who controlled the land route didn't believe it. Prince Henry of Portugal who controlled the sea route didn't believe it. The poor dumb French and English didn't believe it.

Finally, in desperation, I got face-to-face with the Queen of Spain. That Isabella was one smart cookie. She saw right away that I could deliver the goods and commissioned me three ships. One old story said she had to hock her jewels to buy them, but I don't think that is true. I mean, what are three little ships to the Queen of Spain?

Well, in spite of a bunch of ignorant sailors who saw sea monsters in every fog and the end of the world on every horizon, I kept going and sailed to the Indies.

Not once, but *four* times.

I haven't found much gold yet, but I know they aren't going to tell me where their riches are located. I'll eventually get it out of them—might have to enslave and beat some of them to get the secret. I am a man of vision, the best sailor the world has ever known. I'm quite modest, too.

I knew right where India was and I sailed west.

What's that you say?

I haven't really found India? This is just a "New World"?

Well, I'll never believe it. I set out to get to India, and India is where I landed. I am going to see a Rajah riding up on an elephant any day now.

Hey, it's going to happen. I'm Christopher Columbus, Admiral of the Ocean Seas.

Brag of Francis Scott Key

Did you know that I, Francis Scott Key, am the one who wrote the words of the Star Spangled Banner?

Yes, yes, I'm talking about *THE* United States National Anthem.

My words have power.

When you hear, "Oh Say Can You See," don't you immediately stop what you're doing, stand, solemnly place your right hand over your heart, and belt out MY lyrics? My song is performed at football games, baseball games, all kinds of sporting events, and during patriotic celebrations, always to vigorous applause.

I don't mean to brag, but Beyoncé, Whitney Houston, and even *the* Aretha Franklin have sung the words that I wrote. Pretty impressive, right?

I wrote the Star-Spangled Banner way back in 1814, while the War of 1812 waged. I don't mean to boast, but I'm not just a great writer, I'm also a brave man. I penned those words after Washington D.C. was torched by British soldiers. The Capitol, Treasury, and President James Madison's house went up in absolute flames. Burned to the ground! Those Brits wreaked havoc on us Americans.

Then, the British soldiers took a friend of mine hostage to a vessel on the Chesapeake Bay. Well, being such a brave citizen and all, I went out to the ship to negotiate his freedom. Using my savvy attorney skills, I convinced those British scalawags to release him. But before we could leave, nearby Fort McHenry was attacked by the British.

It was September 13, 1814 to be exact. I watched across the harbor as Fort McHenry went up in flames. For twenty-five terrible hours the battle raged. Thousands of soldiers fought. Cannons were lit. Mortar shells were shot.

I was sure we Americans had lost. But then, as the dawn broke, I saw the glorious American flag flying over the fort. The Stars and Stripes flew high.

America prevailed!

Overcome with emotion, I used my brilliant poetry skills to write a few lines about what I'd witnessed. Well, I must be a pretty stellar writer because my brother-in-law, a commander of the militia at Fort McHenry, shared my words and soon it became printed in the *Baltimore Patriot* newspaper.

And the song went viral. Isn't that what you modern folks call something that spreads quickly? Newspapers across the nation printed the poem and it was sung to the melody of a popular song of the day. Everyone LOVED it.

In 1890, the military required that the Star-Spangled Banner be used when the flag was lowered and raised. And in 1931 my little song officially became the National Anthem of the United States.

So next time you hear the Star-Spangled Banner, you should think about our beloved country, but then remember me, Francis Scott Key, a brave attorney and fantastic lyricist.

The Brag of William Dawes Jr.

Perhaps you have never heard of me. I am the forgotten midnight rider.

William Dawes Jr. is my name, and I am quite pleased to make your acquaintance. You probably have heard of my comrade, Paul Revere. Yes, yes, I know what you are thinking.

"Paul Revere, Paul Revere what a bloody, brave, brave lad. Warned everyone that the British were coming. Wasn't he a genius? Wasn't he brave? An absolutely brave genius."

No sense in trying to hide your thoughts. I know that's what you all are thinking. It's what most people think of when they hear the name Paul Revere. Now, I don't mean to embarrass you, but if you think that is all there is to the story you must not be well-educated.

Perhaps, you have relied too much on Wikipedia. I'll let you in on a little secret— Pauly wasn't the only hero that evening. In fact, "hero" seems a bit overrated.

I admit that Paul did ride out that chilly evening of April 18, 1775 and issue warnings that the British had arrived. But, Longfellow rather inaccurately exaggerated Paul's virtues and left readers to ponder the identity of the "friend" referred to in the verses.

Longfellow should have titled the poem: "The Midnight Ride of William Dawes Jr. and Paul Revere." Honestly, "The Midnight Ride of William Dawes Jr." would suit me just fine.

I would like to go on the record by saying that I was the glue that held the mission together and I deserve billing. I'm tired of being left out. Revere was not the only brave soul.

Why, without me, Samuel Adams and John Hancock might have never known that the British were launching an attack.

Without me, the colonies might have not won that initial battle.

Without me, the American Revolution might have gotten off to a rocky start.

Without me, we could all be sitting around sipping tea and speaking funny.

Without me, we might still be under British control and paying their overpriced taxes. But no, none of that occurred. Why? Because I bravely mounted and rode my galloping horse all the way from Boston to Lexington. I successfully warned my fellow patriots that the Regulars were coming. Adams and Hancock were quite happy that I warned them of the impending attack. Old Sam and John patted me on the back and told me thank you.

I don't quite understand, but somehow Pauly gained all the fame and glory. However, I am the real hero. I'm extremely proud of that fact and so is my mother. But, I'm no gloat.

I'm not all about pomp and circumstance.

I'd rather have a bit more humble glory. Gracious, I'm just thankful some old man didn't write an untrue poem about me. Poetry…why that fodder is the stuff of fools.

But, now you know the whole story. You know that I, William Dawes Jr. am one of the true heroes of the American Revolution. The forgotten hero. The forgotten midnight rider.

The Brag of Mount Rushmore

Rushmore's my name; getting carved is my game.

I can honestly say that I am the most famous National Memorial in both the Dakotas. Nearly three million visitors come to see me each year, not counting dogs and cats, which, by the way, are "no-no's." I mean guide dogs can visit, but not just any old animal can see my beauty.

I'm impressive just on my own, but I've also got all this great nature around me. The gorgeous Black Hills are my background.

I am known for my gigantic sixty-foot high granite carvings of the first four fabulous, and I do mean FINE presidents. I got your first president, the one, the only GW. I got your Louisiana Purchasin', Independence Declarin' Tom Jefferson. Then, I got that log splittin', stove top hat wearin' Abe, who kept the country from fallin' apart. Plus, I got the BIG STICK, soft talk man himself, Teddy Roosevelt. As you can see, we are all so close we refer to each other by our nicknames.

Now, if I was going to choose my own name, I'd have picked what Lakota Sioux called me— "Six Grandfathers." That sounds a bit classier than "Mount Rushmore." Of course, I know that Charles E. Rushmore was a New York lawyer, but who wants to be named after a lawyer?

Anyhow, I stand tall. I am 5,725 feet tall!

I admit that carving those dead presidents' faces into my side started out just to increase tourism. But Cal Coolidge and Congress gave it their blessing, so a famous sculptor named Guston Borgium, his son, and 400 other guys spent fourteen years carving those presidents. They started in 1927 and were mostly finished by 1941.

Borgium practiced on some faces at Stone Mountain in Georgia before he got to me. I wouldn't have wanted some guy without any experience taking a pick at my splendor. Borgium chose me because I was a grand looking mountain that faced southeast. I mean politics were involved, but I don't want to go into that. We don't have all day.

Since 1933 I have been part of the National Park Service. For a guy my size, I was a bargain. I cost less that a mill' to make—$989,992.32 to be exact. Okay, okay! I admit an additional ninety-eight million dollars went into upgrading me in 1998.

My biggest boast is that with all the climbing involved, not one single worker died during my carving period.

Today I've got sidewalks, a Visitor Center, a museum, and the Presidential Trail. They have to send mountain climbers up all the time to keep my cracks sealed, but they let me keep my lichens for character.

I've only had one bath—a free clean-up by a German company who used pressurized water at over 200 degrees Fahrenheit. That was hot, but I deserved a spa day.

I'm also a bit of a movie star. Oh yeah! The fans loved me in *Superman II* and *Mars Attack*. My most memorable role was co-starring Cary Grant in Alfred Hitchcock's *North by North West*. I even had a whole movie set as my stunt double in that film.

What? Nothing recent you say?

Well, in granite years I'm still a child star.

The Brag of Chicago

I'm Chicago! Chi! Chicago-land! Chi-town! The Windy City!

The poet Carl Sandburg called me the "City of Big Shoulders," "Hog butcher of the world, stacker of wheat, player with rail roads, storm, husky, brawling City of Big Shoulders" man, that's poetry!

Most great places need to have some great origin myth to make them feel grand. Not me! I am a town without need of a beginning myth, but I had a beginning, all right. Every place does.

I started out as a small fort but an important one.

Location! Location! Location!

Of course, I am ideally located.

Not long after the Americans and British fought over me in the Revolutionary War, I began to bustle with activity. The trade center of the Midwest is what I became. I got Abraham Lincoln elected President. Why, even the story of how a fire gutted me became important—a dumb cow and a lit lantern is all it took to send me ablaze! The Great Fire of 1873 had people around the world talking.

That fire would have finished off some cities but not me! Twenty years later and I was bigger and better than ever, even becoming the showcase of the World Exposition in 1893. It was there that Juicy Fruit gum and Aunt Jemima syrup were introduced. By then, they were calling me the "White City" because I was a beauty.

People looked at me with awe. I was a wonder city.

Millions flocked from around the world to see me. Frederick Jackson Turner, one great historian and a heck of a guy, said Chi-Town was the ONLY place to read his history-rocking paper about the closing of the frontier. Fermi split his atom, and I became the showplace of modernization and beauty. It was even in my city where the United States first automobile race was held. New Yorkers may want to call me the Second City, but I am legendary what with gangsters like Al Capone and Elliot Ness using my turf!

Today, I am home to the best mass transit system in the U.S, the tallest building in the U.S., not to mention I am home to the Chicago Bulls NBA team and baseball's famous Cubs and White Socks. Don't forget about my world famous Chicago Style Pizza. That is definitely major league!

I have a world famous zoo, world famous museums, and two international airports. Plus, President Barack Obama and Oprah Winfrey call me home. No wonder Sinatra sang, "My kind of town, Chicago is!"

The Brag of Harriet Tubman

The slaves called me Moses, and Moses I was.

I truly led them from their slavery and abuse to the promised land of freedom even though I was born a slave myself. When I was in my early teens, a white overseer threw a weight at my head because I tried to protect another slave. The injury left me with seizures for the rest of my life, but I didn't let that or anything else stop me. I did not!

I began the work of my life at twenty-nine years of age by freeing myself. I ran away alone from Maryland to Pennsylvania.

I was not content just being free; I wanted to free my whole family. So, I went right to work on the Underground Railroad. I freed my brothers and my sisters, all their children, and even my old Mammy and Pappy. It took me eight years to do it, but I freed them all. I freed hundreds of others, too!

Here is how I did it.

I would sneak to the woods with my big gun. Then, I would sing out with the sweet loud voice the good Lord gave me. Those slaves out in the field would hear, "Swing Low, Sweet Chariot" comin' out from out in the woods, and they would know that "Moses" was there.

Come night, they would slip away. I led them in the dark, hiding when we needed to. Sometimes those slaves I freed got so scared they wanted to give up, but I wouldn't let them! Freedom was what they wanted, and I was going to see to it that they got it!

To me, the only other choice was that we would all die trying.

I can't count the trips I made back into the slave states. I was a little woman, mind you, not more than five feet tall and small boned, too. But, I had the courage of the lion, the shrewdness of the fox, and the strength of ten thousand in the righteousness of my cause.

When the war came, I, the little bitty black woman that I was, became one of the best scouts the Union army had. I went behind those Confederate lines when brave men would not. And after the Civil War, I just kept working. I collected clothes and food and shoes for the black children. I helped make places where the old and sick could live out their lives free and taken care of. I never quit! But then, you wouldn't expect the woman they called Moses to ever, ever, ever, give up would you?

Well, Moses I was, and Moses I will always be to my people.

The Brag of Phobee Ensminger Burn and the 19th Amendment

Hello. It is so very nice to meet you. My name is Phobee Ensminger Burn, but please call me Feb. I'm a college-educated woman who also knows how to milk a cow, mend clothes, and cook a delicious meal.

After my husband passed away, I had to learn how to take care of the farm, the house, and all matters in between. But amidst all the day-to-day work I make sure to read the newspapers, magazines, and stay abreast of current issues.

But my greatest accomplishment in life is raising my son up right. My little Harry certainly became a history-maker.

It was my son, Harry T. Burn, who helped give all you women the right to vote. It was his single vote that helped ratify the 19th amendment to the United States Constitution.

Hard to believe that women didn't always get the privilege of voting. But some people thought women to be inferior and not smart enough to voice their opinion. Hmmmf. Why I read better than most of the men in my town.

But voting rights changed in 1920, and it's all because my son followed the advice of his dear old mama.

My darling son, Harry, was over in the state capital of Nashville serving as a State Representative. The Tennessee Senate had just passed a resolution in favor of ratification. All needed was the House to vote aye and women across the nation would have the right to vote.

All eyes were glued to Tennessee politics. Thirty-five states had already voted in favor of the amendment, but thirty-six states were needed to make the amendment become law.

People wearing red roses were strolling around Nashville protesting suffrage. Folks wearing yellow roses were sauntering around marching for suffrage.

It was a heated battle.

I hate to say it, but my son was wearing a red rose on his jacket lapel. The House was divided on the issue. Two votes had already been taken leading to a virtual tie. Both times my son voted anti-suffragist.

But then the vote came up again. My son said he was sweatin' something awful. In the room, there was a tie--forty-eight votes for suffrage, forty-eight against.

My son was to cast the tie-breaking vote.

Beneath the red-rose my son felt a hand-written letter in his breast pocket. It was a letter I had sent him. In it I said, " Hurray and vote for Suffrage and don't keep them in doubt." A few lines later I said, "Don't forget to be a good boy and help Mrs. Catt with her "Rats."

Well, I can proudly stand here and say that my son followed my advice. He voted in favor of suffrage!

Some people were thrilled, while others were aghast. Why Harry had to hide out in hotel to escape the violent anger of the anti-suffragists. He even had to have a bodyguard. Some men called him a traitor to all man-kind.

But I consider him a hero. He did what any boy should do—follow the advice of his mama. The day after the amendment passed Harry said, "I believe in full suffrage as a right. I believe we had a moral and legal right to ratify. I know that a mother's advice is always safest for her boy to follow, and my mother wanted me to vote for ratification."

Yes, I am one very proud mama.

SONGS & RAPS

"W, X, Y and Z. Next time won't you sing with me?"

Most people learn the letters of the alphabet and numbers through the aid of songs. Music can be used in a variety of ways to add dramatic impact and enjoyment in the class. Songs can help make events, people, and concepts memorable. Students will gain knowledge by performing and writing songs using social studies content.

Ideas for Using Songs in the Classroom:

Sing-Off/Rap-Off: Students in the classroom sing their written songs aloud for all to hear.

Choral Sing: All students in the classroom sing the song aloud. Everyone has fun and build fluency while singing the song.

Anticipatory Set: Perform songs at the beginning of a unit to build excitement about the subject.

Transition Time: Have the words to the song projected in the room for all to sing during transition time.

Music Video: As an extended project, invite students to create a simple music video for the song they write.

WRITING SONGS & RAPS

Time to get your groove on!

Choose a historical figure, geographical location, event, or inanimate historical object and write a song about the topic. Use the blanks provided to pen some ideas you might have before your write your final project.

STEPS TO TAKE:

1. Choose a historical figure, geographic location, event, or inanimate historical object (i.e. building, artifact, or vehicle).

Topic ideas:

2. Think of a song that has a recognizable beat. You might choose a classic children's song, country song, old school rock, or rap...anything that has a beat where you can sing along. It is a good idea to write down the words of the original song so that you can closely keep the same number of words and syllables for each verse.

Song ideas:

3. Find some interesting facts about your topic and begin thinking how you can turn it into a song. Remember, a song usually tells a story.

A few facts to include:

4. Use facts to compose your song. This may be challenging at first. Don't give up! It might be easier to start with writing a catchy chorus. Then, write the verses.

Catchy chorus:

"Rock Around the Bill of Rights" Song

One, two, three rights, four rights, rock,
Five, six, seven rights, eight rights, rock,
Nine, ten, the Bill of Rights, amendments that rock,
We're gonna rock with the Bill of Rights tonight.

Remember your rights and join me, hon,
We'll have some fun with ev'ry one,
We're gonna rock around our Bill of Rights,
We're gonna rock, rock, rock, 'till we see the light.
We're gonna rock, gonna rock, around the Bill of Rights.

With Amendment one, two, three, and four,
Comes freedom of religion, of speech and more,
We can bear our arms, says the Bill of Rights,
You don't have to keep soldiers at your house all night.
No undue search or seizure, says the Bill of Rights.

Well, Amendment five and Amendment six,
We are guaranteed a trial that can't be fixed.
We don't have to witness against ourselves,
We get speedy public trials, don't sit on the shelves.
We're gonna rock, gonna rock, around the Bill of Rights.

Well, Amendment seven and also eight,
Are to keep us safe from an unfair state.
If we want a jury trial, we've got the right,
No punishments that are out of sight
We're gonna rock, gonna rock, around the Bill of Rights
We end with Amendments nine and ten,

Then we'll rock around the Bill of Rights again.

Nine guarantees the rest of our rights,

Ten says what powers are the states' delights.

We're gonna rock, gonna rock, around the Bill of Rights.

"King George III And The American Revolution" Rap

KING GEORGE III

My dear ungrateful children....

My name is King George , III (PRONOUNCED Aye, Aye, Aye)
I wanna hold on to my slice of the American pie.
You said you hated the Stamp Act, didn't want a stamp tax,
I said, "that's okay," and I gave it the axe!
To the Townshend Act too, you said, "No, and that's that!"
I said "I'll keep on tryin' taxes 'til I got it down pat!"
So, I taxed your sugar, and I taxed your tea,
But what did ya do? Ya threw a tea par-tee.

So now Rebels, stop your fussin' and cease your fightin',
All you Yankee doodlers do is go gripe, gripe, gripin'.
I'll keep you in the empire, yeah, you know I will,
I'll do whatever it takes, so you might as well chill.

You can go on off to Philly, write your dec-laration
I'll just send a few more armies for the Rebel sit-uation
Cause my name is King George, Aye, Aye! Aye!
I'll just come and get my slice of your American pie!

JOHN ADAMS, BEN FRANKLIN, THOMAS JEFFERSON, & JOHN HANCOCK RAP IN REPLY

When in the course of human events....

JOHN ADAMS

Hey, old King George! Here's what we say to you:
In America, you're done, you're through!
We've got our own George now; his name is Washington!
He'll be kickin' out kings and he'll be havin' some fun!

BEN FRANKLIN

We're hangin' together; so we won't hang alone;
Startin' now, our America's a "no King zone"!
With our muskets, some cannon and a little help from France!
You'll be out of here, King, in an exit dance.

TOM JEFFERSON

These truths are so self-evident,
Instead of kings, we'll have a president.
George I I I, yo, don't you see.
All men are equal and we will be free.

JOHN ADAMS, BEN FRANKLIN, & TOM JEFFERSON TOGETHER

We'll make a declaration, which the Congress will pass,
You're out King George, don't give us any sass.
We will list all the bad, bad things you've done,
So you better take your redcoats and you better run.

JOHN HANCOCK

I'm gonna sign it first and I'll write real big!
Take that, King George and stick it in your wig!
And a piece of this pie, King. Oh my, no!
Shut the door behind you as you go.

ALL

Shut the door behind you as you go!

"Father Abraham Lincoln" Rap

Father Abraham (Pum! Pum!) Father Abraham (Pum! Pum!)
If you can't hold this land together, no one can! (Pum! Pum!)
Father Abraham (Pum! Pum!) Father Abraham (Pum! Pum!)
If you can't hold this land together, no one can! (Pum! Pum!)

Here comes this long, tall lanky man, out from Illinois.
He got elected in a four-way race—what a mess, oh boy!
He got the South mad, lookin' sad, cause of slavery
They said it was a shame; they thought his aim was to set slaves free.

REPEAT CHORUS

That brought Fort Sumter, what a number and then the Southern states secede.
Then on the battle field, the Union reeled, boys in blue could not succeed.
Abe tried a whole slew of generals; not one of them could stand!
Cause all those Federals with medals, huh! They just didn't have the sand!

REPEAT CHORUS

While all those Generals kept claimin', "Abe, we just can't!"
From out in Vicksburg, Chattanooga along came Grant.
At Spotsylvania and Cold Harbor Lee was backtrackin', givin' ground,
And retreat from Petersburg assured the South was going down.

REPEAT CHORUS

"Thomas Alva Edison" Rap

Thomas Alva Edison! That's my name.
Creatin' and Inventin' until the world's not the same!
With the incandescent lightbulb I won my fame!
A thousand, ninety-two more patents—that's not lame!

I was the razzle, dazzle, schazzle, frazzle wizard of Menlo Park.

I went on a spree to tree electricity,
But when I see the key was no mystery.
I did my wizardry, I was a whizz you see,
So I tinkered and concocted makin' history!

I was the razzle, dazzle, schazzle, frazzle wizard of Menlo Park.

As a boy I was a whiz kid, an eager beaver,
Til I got taken down with scarlet fever.
I had no doubt, I would win out, I was a true believer,
That I'd do great things, get rich—ca-ching, I had inventin' fever.

I was the razzle, dazzle, schazzle, frazzle wizard of Menlo Park.

But I overcame, got in the game, things will never be the same.
I fought back up, got back up, stood back up, kept up with what came.
I wouldn't strike out till I won out and I made myself a name.
I did sound, light, cameras, changed the entertainment game.

I was the razzle, dazzle, schazzle, frazzle wizard of Menlo Park.

"I Have a Dream" Rap

I'm Martin Luther King and I've got a dream;

I remembered "My Country 'Tis of Thee"

How things don't have to stay the way they seem.

Let freedom ring, everyone should be free.

I talked about the Emancipation Proclamation and finally I said let's leave the past

About discrimination and segregation. Let America be free at last!

I brought up the bank of justice, too. "Thank God Almighty we are free at last!"

I have a dream how we'll live our creed;

"All created equal" will be believed.

I have a dream, how the girls and boys

Will all hold hands in American joy.

I dream of a land where we judge no one

By the color of their skin, cause oppression's no fun!

"The Great Space Race" Song
To the tune of "The Farmer in the Dell"

The great space race begins,
The great space race begins,
Up, up, to outer space
Who is going to get to the moon?

1957

The Soviets launch Sputnik,
The Soviets launch Sputnik,
Up, up, to outer space
A satellite is sent.

1958

The Americans launch Explorer I,
The Americans launch Explorer I,
Up, up, to outer space,
A satellite is sent.

The Americans form NASA,
The Americans form NASA,
Up, up, to study space
A federal agency is created.

1959

The Soviets launch Luna II,
The Soviets launch Luna II,
Up, up, to outer space
The space probe hits the moon!

1961

The Soviets send Yuri to space,
The Soviets send Yuri to space,
Up, up, to outer space
The cosmonaut orbits the Earth.

Alan Shepard Jr. goes to space,
Alan Shepard Jr. goes to space,
Up, up, to outer space
The Americans send an astronaut to space.

1962

John Glenn, Jr. orbits the Earth,
John Glenn, Jr. orbits the Earth,
Up, up, to outer space
The Americans send another astronaut to space.

1963

Valentina Tereshkova goes to space,
Valentina Tereshkova goes to space,
Up, up, to outer space
The Soviets send a woman to space.

1968

The Americans send Apollo 8 to space,
The Americans send Apollo 8 to space,
Up, up, to outer space
A manned spacecraft orbits the moon.

1969

The Americans make it to the moon,
The Americans make it to the moon,
Up, up, to outer space,
Buzz, Michael, and Neil make it to the moon.

Neil Armstrong walks on the moon,
Neil Armstrong walks on the moon,
Up, up, to outer space,
Neil Armstrong walks on the moon!

The great space race is over,
The great space race is over,
Up, up, to outer space,
The Americans walked on the moon.

CADENCES

*"Washington with his big white hair;
hatched a plan to cross the Delaware!"*

The military uses cadences to keep in step. You can use cadences to help you learn historical information. In a cadence, a leader says no more than ten syllables in a line for everyone to repeat. It is called a "call-and-response" verse. Sometimes, the last word in each line rhymes; but that isn't necessary.

Ideas for Using Cadences in the Classroom:

March to the Beat: Start or end class with a marching cadence. Students can march in place at their seats for exercise.

Anticipatory Set: Perform cadences at the beginning of a unit to build excitement about the subject.

Transition Time: Have a leader led a cadence during transition time.

Daily Cadence: Each day of the week, have a minute of class devoted to a student leading a student written cadence.

WRITING CADENCES

I don't know but I've been told; Antarctica is mighty cold!

Choose a historical figure, geographical location, event, or inanimate historical object and write a cadence about the topic. Use the blanks provided to pen some ideas you might have before your write your final project.

STEPS TO TAKE:

1. Choose a historical figure, geographic location, event, or inanimate historical object (i.e. building, artifact, or vehicle).

Topic ideas:

2. Choose some facts about the subject that you want to include in your cadence.

A few facts to include:

3. Begin turning those facts into seven- or eight-syllable lines for people to repeat (at least try to keep it under ten syllables). Your cadence doesn't have to tell a story, but it should follow a logical pattern.

Lines to include:

4. After writing your sample lines see if you can make the end words rhyme. You can use a poetry pattern.

5. Create your final cadence. Then, get some friends together and have everyone march to your beat.

Rural, Suburban, Urban

300 mil' plus populate the U.S
Where we live is what we'll address.

Urban is a big city
Filled with lots of large buildings
New York, San Fran, and Chicago
Are all urban places I'd like to go.

Suburbs are the outskirts of a large town
Filled with schools, homes, and shopping all around
Neighborhoods and children on bikes
This is an area I could like.

Rural areas are populated less
Lots of land defines this place
Grasslands, prairies, and farmland
Lots of space is so grand.

Urban, rural, and suburban
Wherever you live is great I'm certain.

Continents

North and South America
Europe and Antarctica:
Africa and Asia, yes.
And Australia too I guess.
They are continents we know.
All around them oceans flow.

Latitude and Longitude

Latitude and longitude help us tell location
Seen as lines on maps and globes
That crisscross seas and oceans.

Latitude goes north and south
Longitude runs east and west.

Latitude lines are parallels
Like the tropics and equator.

Longitude lines are horizontal
Running from side to side.

Africa

Africa's a continent;
Many climates it presents.
Deserts, mountains, plains, and lakes
Not just jungles, goodness sakes.

Many nations, fifty-two,
Animals we see in zoos.
Places torn by hunger, strife,
And disease that ruins life.

Africa has great spots too,
Things to see and things to do.
Kilimanjaro, ancient walls,
The Zambezi basin, Victoria Falls.

Eli Whitney Cadence

Eli Whitney was a young man with a plan;
To invent machines that really ran.
That did work faster, made things better;
Our Eli was a real go-getter.

Eli Whitney invented the cotton gin,
To take seeds out, not leave them in.
He made "Cotton King" in the South;
Well, kiss my grits and shut my mouth.

Then Eli turned to making guns;
For safety, that's how wars are won.
He made each part interchangeable;
From barrel to stock and trigger pull.

Daniel Boone Cadence

Dan'l Boone was a trailblazer, hunter, and so much more.
He commanded the militia in the Revolution's War;
Fought the Shawnee, the Chickasaw, the Cherokee, and more.
And he showed a few "bars" what a rifle was for!

With "Kaintuck" settled, folks all around;
Daniel Boone took off for wilder ground.
Took off for Missouri where room could be found;
With this family, his flintlock, and his good old hound.

Underground Railroad Cadence

It hasn't got a whistle;
Doesn't go Choo Choo,
But in the dark of the night
It's coming through!

It's the Underground Railroad;
And it's heading on north,
To Canada, Chicago
Or old New York!

Come on and follow
That woman Moses;
It won't be easy,
No bed of roses.

Swing low, sweet chariot;
Ride the freedom train!
Through the woods and down the rivers;
Up north to liberty lane.

Harriet Beecher Stowe Cadence

A famous woman you ought to know;
Was a mother and writer called Harriet B. Stowe.
Raised seven sons; they all were preachers,
She didn't like any of slavery's features.

Uncle Tom's Cabin was a book she wrote;
Against slavery, it got the vote.
Its readers all felt sympathy
For slaves, but not for the horrible institute of slavery.

Clara Barton Cadence

It is no mystery,
Clara Barton is a famous woman in American history.

During the Civil War she risked her life
to help wounded soldiers who'd been shot by a gun or stabbed with a knife.

She went to the very front of the battlefield,
During danger she did not yield.

Across the globe she would go
Helping people—she's a true hero.

The American Red Cross she did start
Encouraging other people to do their part.

Providing disaster relief to those in need
Delivering food and shelter is part of their creed.

Thank you Ms. Barton for your life filled with bravery and integrity,
You've left such a big legacy.

At the Alamo Cadence

Two hundred Texans
Died at the Alamo
Defending freedom
Against 5,000 foe.
Crocket, Travis, Bowie fought bravely till the end
Defending that small mission; knowing they could not win.

Then at San Jacinto,
Sam Houston won the day;
Captured Santa Anna
Whose army ran away.
Sam charged in shouting, "Remember the Alamo."
And Texas independence was won that day.

Teddy Roosevelt Cadence

Explorer, soldier, and Pres –i –dent;
TR was one who said just what he meant.
In Old New York he became top cop;
And brought corruption to a stop.

The youngest "pres" at forty two;
Bustin' Trusts was something he wanted to do.
Won the Peace Prize given by Nobel;
And he built the Panama Canal.

Cuban Missile Crisis

With our missiles trained on him
Krushchev came up with a plan;
He'd give Castro some of theirs,
And give Kennedy a scare.

Kennedy said we'll blockade,
Cut off imports, exports, aid.
Khrushchev said you've gone too far,
We won't stand it; this means war.

In the end diplomacy
Saved us from a missile spree.
Cuban missiles were removed;
Ours in Turkey pulled back too.

This was part of the Cold War;
No one then quite knew the score.
Fear and propaganda spread.
Some thought we'd all end up dead.

A-bombs, H-Bombs, Satellites,
Atomic subs and missile sites,
Lasted nearly forty years.
When it ended, we all cheered.

CLASS ACTION STORIES

Class Action stories are readers' theater plays in which multiple performers are involved. The story-like script has signal words that cause readers to perform an action or say something specific. Students don't even have to leave their seats to be involved. Class Action Stories help students develop fluency, vocabulary skills, and develop familiarity with a story.

Ideas for Using Class Action Stories in the Classroom:

Choral Class Action: A narrator reads the story aloud, and the rest of the class acts out the remaining roles.

Character Class Action: Everyone is assigned a part to the story and acts out their roles.

WRITING CLASS ACTION STORIES

Be bard for the day!

You are going to write an interactive play for your class to perform. Turn a great story from history into a fun drama. Use the blanks provided to pen some ideas you might have before your write your final project.

STEPS TO TAKE:

1. Choose a great event from history to condense into short class action story. The event will be the basis of the plot.

Event ideas:

2. Write a quick summary of your chosen story. This way you can identify potential characters. The character may not necessarily be one person but could be an emotion or group of people.

Write down a quick summary and underline the characters:

3. Create one action for each character. Each time the character is mentioned the person (or people) playing the character will perform that action. Have fun creating the actions (singing a song, saying a chant, making a motion, etc.). Actions can be kooky but make sure they go along with the story.

Characters and actions:

4. Write the final script in an entertaining story form. Note: It is helpful to underline the characters.

5. Performance time! Assign the parts, and then read the story aloud. Everyone can read the story chorally (with the characters performing their actions) or a narrator can read the story aloud (and the characters perform their actions). Have fun!

Pocahontas: A Class Action Story

When the Reader Reads:	You say/do this:	When the Reader Reads:	You say/do this:
CHIEF POWATAN/ POWATAN	Slowly raise right hand and assert: *"I'm in charge here!"*	**POCAHONTAS**	Simper: *"Little snow feather."*
SHIP	Shout: *"Sail Ho!"*	**ENGLISH/ ENGLISHMEN**	In your most aristocratic English voice say: *"I do believe it's tea time!*
CAPTAIN JOHN SMITH	Strut and brag saying, *"I can take care of myself!"*	**SWAMP, SWAMPY**	Reach up and shout, *"I'm sinking, I'm sinking!"*
RIVERS/STREAMS	Go: *"Burble, burble."*		

Pocahontas was the daughter of the mighty **Chief Powatan**. Her name meant "playful one." **Pocahontas** had another name, too. It was "Little Snow Feather," and only her many little brothers and sisters knew this secret name. As a little girl, **Pocahontas** loved to play with her siblings.

Pocahontas's people were also called the **Powatans**. They lived in what we now call Virginia. The **Powatan** land had rushing **streams and rivers** full of fish and beautiful thick woods full of animals. It also had dangerous **swamps**. **Pocahontas** and her people lived in houses made from bending together young trees and weaving branches in and out to make a thick hatch.

When **Pocahontas** was ten-years-old, three **ships** with large white sails appeared over the horizon and sailed up the beautiful **river.** The **Powatans** had never seen anything like these **ships** or the strange men on them before. They thought the **ships** were floating islands.

The **Powatans** wanted to know what the strangers were doing in **Powatan** country. When the **Englishmen** came off their ships, the **Powatans** were able to see these strange people up close. The **Englishmen** had hair on their faces, and they wore very strange clothes. **Pocahontas** and her friends couldn't help giggling at how funny the **Englishmen** looked.

The **Englishmen** began chopping down trees to build forts and houses. They built a whole village and called it Jamestown. Some **Powatans** traded corn with the **English** strangers for shiny things of glass and metal like beads, bells, and mirrors. Other **Powatans** were worried because the **Englishmen** seemed to be planning to stay in their land and not sail back in their great **ships**.

The leader of the **Englishmen** was a hairy-faced man whose name was **Captain John Smith**. **Captain Smith** let everyone know that he was very brave. **Captain John Smith** told a story about one cold winter day when he went hunting alone with one **Powatan** to guide him across the **streams and rivers** and through the **swamps**. As they were walking near one **swampy** area, a shower of arrows came flying through the air.

Captain John Smith couldn't see where the arrows came from, but he held his **Powatan** guide in front of himself as a shield and tried to run away. But **Captain John Smith** stumbled over a tree root and fell into an icy **swamp**. The **Powatan** guide pulled **Captain John Smith** out of the **swamp**.

The guide built a fire and warmed the cold **Englishman**. After **Captain John Smith** got dry and warm, the **Powatan** guide took the **Englishman** to see **Pocahontas's** father, Chief **Powatan.** The **Powatans** pretended to be friendly and provided **Captain John Smith** a feast of roasted deer meat, corn, and turkey to celebrate his being saved from the **swamp**.

Suddenly, right in the middle of the feast, Chief **Powatan** gave a signal and **Captain John Smith** was thrown to the ground by several **Powatan** warriors. One raised a great heavy club and was ready to bash **Captain John Smith's** head. In the nick of time, little **Pocahontas** rushed forward.

She ran in front of all the **Powatan** warriors and threw her arms around **Captain John Smith's** head. Chief **Powatan** shouted a warning and the warrior with the club did not strike. According to **Captain John Smith**, **Pocahontas** saved his life.

We do not know if this story is true or not. **Captain John Smith** told the story, but he was a notorious braggart and many think he was a liar as well. But we do know that **Captain John Smith** explored the forest, the **rivers**, the **streams**, and the **swamps** around Jamestown.

We also know that when she was older, **Pocahontas** married one of the **Englishmen**, a man named John Rolfe. The little **Powatan** princess sailed away on one of the great **ships** of the **Englishmen** all the way to **England** where she got to see the King of all **Englishmen** for herself. **Little Snow Feather** certainly did fly far away from home.

Constitution: A Class Action Story

When the Reader Reads:	You say/do this:	When the Reader Reads:	You say/do this:
UNITED STATES/ UNITED/ GOVERNMENT	Raise pretend flag and quickly shout: *"We the people of the United States."*	**GEORGE WASHINGTON**	Wave and say: *"It's not easy being Father of the Country."*
JAMES MADISON	Do a little dance and sing: *"Central government is the thing! It just needs some bling."*	**CONSTITUTION/ SECRET/ SECRETLY**	Whisper: *"Shh!! It's a secret."*
SOVEREIGN STATES/ STATES	Shout: *"You are not the boss of me!"*	**CONGRESS, DELEGATES, REPRESENTATIVES**	Shout: *"I'm representin'!"*
AMERICANS/ AMERICAN REVOLUTION	Salute while chanting: *"We hold these truths to be self-evident, that all men are created equal."*	**COMPROMISE**	Shrug and say: *"Ya give a little; ya take a little."*
DEBATE	Make a peace sign and say: *"Can't we stop all this arguing?"*	**KING**	Shake fist, shouting: *"King! Schming! Who needs a king?"*

The **American Revolution** was over, and **America** was free from **Britain** at last. We called ourselves the **United States**, but that did not mean the **states** were really **united**. In fact, the **states** like to call themselves **sovereign states,** meaning that each **state** was its own boss.

    George Washington and many **other Americans** worried about this because they knew that no **state** was strong enough to survive by itself. **George Washington** frowned on the idea of **states** being **sovereign** over the **national government**. So did others like John Adams of Massachusetts, Ben Franklin of Pennsylvania, Alexander Hamilton of New York, and **James Madison** of Virginia.

More than any other delegate, **Madison** believed that the government of **America** under the Confederation gave too much emphasis on **states'** sovereignty and not enough to national **government**.

Many members of **Congress** believed that to be a **united** country, **Americans** should have a **king**. Some thought that Frederick, **King** George's second son would be a good **king**. Others believed that **George Washington** should be **king**. However, **George Washington** did not want to be **king**, nor did he believe **America** should have a **king**. Many members of **Congress** thought that we had just fought the **American Revolution** to get rid of **a king**, but most agreed that **America** needed a stronger central government.

By the spring of 1787, enough people thought that the **United States** needed to be more **united**. A **constitutional** convention was called. All thirteen **states** secretly sent **delegates** to Philadelphia to write a new **Constitution** for a more **united** America. The **delegates** elected **George Washington** to be president of the convention and to write a new **constitution**. But it was **James Madison** who was the real Father of the **Constitution**.

There was a lot of **debate** at the **constitutional** convention. The big **states** had one plan, called the Virginia Plan that favored big **states**. The small **states** had another plan, called the New Jersey Plan that favored small **states**. There were a lot of other plans, and the **delegates debated** long and hard.

George Washington was frustrated. Finally, the delegates found a way to **compromise**. There would be two houses of **Congress** in the new government. The upper house would have two **representatives** from each **state,** and the other house would have **representatives** based on the population of the various **states.**

Slowly, through the long hot summer, the **delegates debated** and hammered out the new plan of **government**. They decided on a president as a position where one would be a strong executive but who could not make laws. They decided on how we would vote for the president, what the Supreme Court would be like, and all the major features of the **American government**.

Finally, on September 17, 1789, the final draft of the **Constitution** was signed by thirty-nine of the fifty-five people who attended the convention. Some people had left early, while some refused to sign. The **delegates** who signed were proud. They created the **Constitution**—a new kind of government. On the day of the adjournment, Benjamin Franklin said that it was possible that no better document could have been created.

Hey Chief! Let's Dump the Tea: A Class Action Story

When the Reader Reads:	You say/do this:	When the Reader Reads:	You say/do this:
BRITISH	*"Cheerio! Pip, Pip!"*	**AMERICA OR AMERICAN**	Sing: *"God Bless America."*
COLONISTS OR COLONIES	*"Independency!"*	**LEXINGTON AND CONCORD**	Shout: *"Did you hear that shot?"*
SUGAR TAX OR SUGAR	*"Sweeeet!"*	**ANGRY OR ANGRIER**	*"Them's fightin' laws!"*
STAMP ACT	*"You can stick it!"*	**BOSTON**	Sing: *"Gonna have a party!"*
TEA	*"One lump, or two?"*	**SHIPS**	Shout: *"Sail HO!"*
TAX(ES)	*"Money, money—give the King your money!"*		

By 1775, when the "shot heard 'round the world" was fired at **Lexington and Concord**, the **British** had tried every way they could think of to collect **taxes** from the **colonists** to help pay for the cost of the French and Indian War. They tried a **Sugar Tax** which **taxed** everything made from **sugar**. The **Colonists** didn't have a taste for the **Sugar Act**, but the **tax** the **colonists** hated the most was the **Stamp Act**.

The **Stamp Act** law called for a tax on all printed things—deeds, letters, birth records, stationary, and even playing cards. The **Stamp Act** made the **colonists** really, really **angry**. Samuel Adams led the opposition in Boston, a group called the Sons of Liberty, who minced no words about how **angry** they were.

Finally, the **colonists** told the **British** to get rid of the **Stamp Act,** but the **British** government still thought it had the right to **tax** the **American colonists**. The **British** tried to collect one **tax** after another, and each **tax** made the **colonists angrier**, especially those **colonists** in **Boston.**

The people of **Boston** complained so loudly that the **British** government put armed troops in **Boston**. Talk about **angry**! Tension between the **British** soldiers and the **colonists** led to an event called the **Boston** Massacre where five people were killed after an **angry** mob threw some stones at a **British** soldier.

Soon after that, the **British** government removed all but one of the **taxes**. The only **tax** that was left was the **Tea Tax.**

The **colonists sure do** like their **tea,** but they were so **angry** about the **Tea Tax** that they started an anti-**tea** movement. Many **colonists** pledged to drink local herbs rather than **British tea**. This anti-**tea** movement caused the **British** East India Company that sold the **tea** to lose money. To protect the **British** East India Company, which had a lot of investors in the **British** parliament, the **British** government passed the **Tea** Act of 1773.

The **British** East India **Tea** Company tried to collect the **taxes** from the still **angry colonists**, but the **tax** collectors got nothing.

In September of 1773, seven ships left London carrying 2,000 chests filled with **tea.** The ships were headed for **Boston** in the **America colonies**. The **colonists** knew they were coming and were more than **angry**. Talk of **taxation** without representation spread through the **colonies**.

On November 28, 1773, the first **British** ship was spotted anchoring in the **Boston** harbor. The **colonists** were determined to keep the **tea** from ever reaching a port in **Boston**. They immediately went into action when another **British** ship sailed into the harbor. At a **Boston** town meeting, many **colonists** spoke **angrily**. The captains of the **British** ships refused to take the ships out of **Boston** harbor.

The report is that someone in the crowd at the **Boston** Town meeting shouted, "Who knows how well **tea** mingles with sea water?"

By that time it was growing dark outside. A signal was given and loud whoops filled the air. **Colonists** covered in soot and wrapped blankets around their heads to hide their identify swooped down on the ships. Crate after crate of **tea** was broken open with hatchets and dumped over the sides of the ships into the waters of **Boston** Harbor.

This three-hour raid become known as the **Boston Tea** Party.

No one knows for sure which **colonists** took part. Paul Revere may have been one, as may have been Sam Adams. Whoever they were, those **tea**-dumping **Boston colonists** dressed as very unbelievable Indians played an important role in creating an independent **America**.

Don't Forget Philo...: A Class Action Story

When the Reader Reads:	You say/do this:	When the Reader Reads:	You say/do this:
FARNSWORTH, PHILO T. OR PHILO T. FARNSWORTH	*"What's on TV tonight?"*	CARVER	Lick a pretend spoon and say: *"That's really smoooooooth!"* (really draw out the smooth)
INVENTION, INVENTOR, INVENT	Shout: *"Eureka! I've got it!"*	BELL	Pretend to hold a phone and say: *"Talk to me, baby!"*
FRANKLIN	Pretend to touch a hot stove and say: *"Man, is that hot!"*	TWENTY-ONE	Dreamingly sigh: *"Ah, a magical year."*
PATENTS	Shout: *"This invention is MINE."*	HIGH SCHOOL	Sing: *"School days, school days."*
EDISON	Hold up a pretend light-bulb and say: *"Now that's what I call bright!"*	MONEY	*"Ca-ching!"*
TELEVISION	*"Boob tube! Idiot box!"*		

Who was the greatest **inventor** of them all?

Was it **Edison? Bell? Carver? Franklin?**

They were great **inventors**, that is for sure, with hundreds of **patents** among them. **Franklin invented** the **Franklin** stove to warm us. **Carver** gave us peanut butter so we could have a yummy treat. **Edison's invention**, the electric light bulb was enlightening. And **Bell** helped us talk to everyone with the telephone. But for some people's **money**, the greatest **inventor** was **Philo T. Farnsworth**.

Who in the world is **Farnsworth**?

What do you ask did **Philo T. Farnsworth invent** that made him so great?

Philo T. is ultimately responsible for cable, satellite, commercials, Sunday Night Football, DVR, MTV, and all the wonders that appear on our flat screens. Yep, you got it, **Philo. T** was to TV what **Edison** was to the lightbulb, what **Carver** was to the peanut, and what **Bell** was to the telephone. If you wildly guessed that on September 10, 1928 in San Francisco, California **Philo T. Farnsworth invented** the **television** you would be right on the **money**.

Philo. T or Phil, as he liked to be called was born in a log cabin. Really—he was! He rode to high school on horseback. And, wouldn't you know it, young **Farnsworth** was tilling potatoes behind a horse when the idea that an electron beam could scan images the same way, line by line, just as you read a book. That turned out to be key to the **television** picture tube. Needless to say, young **Philo T** did not think like most fourteen-year-olds. But an idea does not a **TV** make, and it took young **Farnsworth** until he was **twenty-one** to develop a working television.

Phil was a smart cookie. After two years of high school, he was admitted to Brigham Young University. He always gave most of the credit for his swift progress to his high school chemistry teacher, Justin Tollman. After high school, **Phil** got busy. By the time he was **twenty-one**, he'd dropped out of school, got married, found investors with **money**, and moved to San Francisco.

On September 27, 1927, **Phil** streamed the first **television** image to people investing in him said, "The darned thing works." Well, that is not quite what they said, but close enough.

Then things turned UGLY!

Money!

RCA, one of America's largest and most powerful corporations, had a scientist working with them who had developed a tube of some kind. RCA had a **patent** and so **Phil** and RCA went to court. For ten years they were entwined in a legal struggle when finally, **Phil** won and RCA agreed to pay **Phil** royalties.

You would think that **Philo** would have been quickly rolling in the **money**, but you would be wrong! By then the Great Depression was in full force and few people had **money**. Then World War II hit and people's **money** went to war and not **television**. It was a very long time before **Phil** collected much **money** on his **television**.

Years later, **Phil** actually appeared on **television**. He was a mystery guest on **a television** program called *What's My Line?* A panel tried to discover what he had done. One of the panelists asked **Phil** if he had **invented** some kind of machine that might be painful when used. **Farnsworth** answered, "Yes. Sometimes it is most painful. I can't stand those commercial breaks."

LETTERS

In the days before e-mail, texting, tweeting, and telephone conversations, people contacted one another with hand-written letters. Penning notes as a historic subject helps writers consider perspectives of particular individuals. Using letters as monologues helps readers and audience members to understand those perspectives. Confession letters, love letters, and fan letters are just some of the formats writers can use to pen a few words from a historic or geographic subject.

Ideas for Using Letters in the Classroom:

Fan Mail: Students in the classroom read their fan letters for all to hear. Encourage students to act extremely excited when they read.

Choral Read: All students in the classroom read a fan letter aloud. Everyone has fun and builds fluency while acting out the excitement of the fan. Discuss why the recipient deserves a fan letter.

Anticipatory Set: Perform fan letters at the beginning of a unit to build excitement and intrigue about the subject.

Vivid Viewpoints: After student performances compare and contrast various viewpoints that were presented.

WRITING FAN LETTERS

You are the man, the woman, the bomb, the schizzle!

Choose a historical figure, geographic location, event, or inanimate historical object and write a fan letter full of flattery. Use the blanks provided to pen some ideas you have before you write your final project.

STEPS TO TAKE:

1. Choose a historical figure, geographic location, event, or inanimate historical object that deserves a fan letter.

Ideas for who needs a bit of flattery:

2. Investigate. Why might you be his or her biggest fan? Write down any background information you find. You will want to use facts in your letter.

Background information:

3. In friendly letter format, write a fan letter from the viewpoint of his or her biggest fan. The letter might be from you or from one historical figure to another. Just don't expect to receive a response letter in the mail anytime soon!

Fan Letter to Leif Eriksson

Dear Mr. Eriksson,

Seriously, you are the BEST, most baddest, freshest Viking EVER! I just want to clear the air by saying I know that you are the one who discovered North America around the year 1000. I'm really not that great at math, but even I can run the digits and figure out that 1000 is quite a bit earlier then when Columbus sailed ocean blue in 1492.

We should be celebrating Eriksson Day not Columbus Day. I heard that you sailed in your cool longship to what we now call Newfoundland in Canada. You called it Vinland. Sweet! I really like that that name.

Just think, the Canadians could be the "Vinians" if we truly celebrated your accomplishments. Instead, most of us just think of you as a brute who drinks out of skulls and wears horned hats. As if! I know neither of those things are true.

I'm going to begin a Columbus boycott and try to petition my friends to join. They need to know the truth about you, Leif.

I really appreciate your efforts of spreading Christianity. Vikings get a bad name, but I know that one of your missions in life was to spread the Good Word. I don't know if it is true or not, but I read that on your trip to Norway, you stayed with King Olaf I. He told you about his conversion from worshipping the Viking gods to worshipping the Christian God.

The testimonial must have been pretty powerful because you, too, became a Christian. You even went back to Greenland (which was covered in ice) and converted your mother. She is the one who built the first Christian Church in Greenland. I'm sure you know all that information about yourself, but just in case you forgot, I thought I'd include it in this letter.

All in all, you don't sound like much of a savage to me (although if you were a brute I'd still be cool with that).

I also really like you because you were born exactly 1,000 years before my granddad. He was born in 1960, and I hear you were probably born in 960. My granddad's name is Eric, and your dad was Erik the Red. I'm seriously thinking we are brothers separated by time. I mean, I like to explore, you like to explore; I'm a Christian, you were a Christian; I discovered a new creek behind my house; you discovered North America. Wow! The similarities are fierce. Holler at me if you ever make it back to America. We should definitely hang out some time.

Your biggest fan,

DERRICK - AGE 10

Fan Letter to Capitalism

Dear Capitalism,

Ka-ching! Yeah, last month I cleared $2,000 of my very own money, and it is all because of you, Capitalism. You see, my Mom and Dad taught me the value of work and turning a profit. Last month I decided it was time for me to make them proud by venturing out into the world of making dough. The kind of dough I'm talking about is even sweeter than cookie dough. I'm talking about cash money!

Mom and Dad taught me that capitalism means a free market economy. In a free market economy, goods and services are exchanged for money. I'm free to do this in America.

I just love how you gave me the freedom to open my own business. I was sure to open it within the confines of the law, and I made sure to give good old Uncle Sam his fair share of taxes (well, I plan on doing that at the end of the year). I mean we all have to follow the laws of the land.

At this point, you are probably asking what type of business an eight-year-old runs that can clear $2,000 in a month. Well, I'm not talking about mowing yards. Mom still won't let me drive.

I'm not talking about a lemonade stand either. I'm not good at the squeezing part.

I'm talking about a neighborhood tabloid magazine.

For my business, I decided to write a simple newsletter that clues readers in on the happenings of my neighborhood. I'm providing both a service and a product. I started out my investigative journalism career by hiding behind the hedges at Mrs. Waters house. I discovered that she was doing her son's homework.

Maybe you aren't interested in that story, but some of the neighbors thought it pretty interesting. Especially because she is all the time bragging about her son's straight "A" report card.

Then, I saw Mr. Richards bring some plumbing company into his house to fix something under the sink while he played video games all afternoon. His wife was especially interested in that story. It seems he told her he had been doing all the handy work at their house.

With articles like that, readership soared. I started selling the newsletter at $5.00 a paper. But then the newsletter really came in demand. People wanted to secretly buy the paper. I offered to discreetly give them the daily news for $10.00!

I sold tons of papers at that price! But then a funny thing happened. People started slipping me money not to report what I had seen outside their houses.

Well, I wasn't one to turn down even a penny, so I took the money. I'm not sure that was really in the confines of the law; I'll have to look into that. All this time, my parents were clueless about my newsletter, which was good because I wanted to surprise them with my profits. But, in a couple of days they found out.

I thought they would have been proud; I was wrong.

Dad yelled a lot and mom cried. It seems some of their friends were angry about what I was reporting. Some of the ladies of neighborhood were especially irate about my daily fashion report where I rated their clothing choices.

I argued, "Hey, people buy the tabloids. I was just trying to turn our neighbors into celebrities."

Mom said I better stop.

Dad said I better stop.

I said that I was just living out the dreams of capitalism.

That is when Dad gave me a BIG speech about ethics. I guess it wasn't very nice of me to comment that Ms. Rivers wore the same sweatpants three days in a row.

So Capitalism, I must say that I adore you because you give me the freedom to make money. However, I've also learned about ethics. I guess I was a bit rude.

Next time I'll try my hand at selling cookies. Maybe I can make dough the good old-fashioned way. I bet Mrs. Smith will buy some of mine—she always purchases store bought cookies. But then she curiously takes them out of the package, puts them on her own plate, and tells everyone she had labored all day baking. Funny! Oh well, to each their own.

Your fan,
LAUREN - AGE 10

Fan Letter to Anne Hutchinson: A Puritan Woman Banished From the Massachusetts Bay Colony

1637

Dear Mistress Hutchison,

I must tell thou that I am thy biggest fan. I am writing this to thee to express my gratitude. But I do hope thou can keep our correspondence private. I know that as Puritan women, we are not heralded for expressing our own thoughts.

As a member of thine's Bible study group, I must say that thee seem to have a close relationship to our God and that thee truly seek to understand His word. I am greatly distressed that thou is under trial for speaking thy beliefs about God.

When my family came to the Massachusetts Bay colony from England, I was under the impression that we would have freedom of religion. I was excited about purifying the Church of England. Secretly I hoped that this would mean women would have the right to think and speak freely about God.

I can tell that this is not the case in our Puritan congregation, although I hope for a better day. I have been mortified that the court and Governor Winthrop has had thee stand trial with thou being with child. This will make thine's fourteenth or fifteenth baby, will it not?

Thou is such an inspiration to me. I wish that I could express my thoughts freely. What, with all the cooking, mending, and gardening that I do I rarely have the opportunity to converse with my neighbors, let alone lead a Bible group such as thyself has accomplished. Thou takes care of all thy children, thy home, and thy husband.

I understand that thou is also a self-educated woman on the subject of theology. That thou reads extensively from thy father's library. Thou seems to do it all and make time to lead so many people in thy Bible group. I have been amazed how large our group has grown. Even men are showing up to listen to thy thoughts! Thou has many fans, although many are fearful of speaking up for thou at this point.

I have heard murmurings that thou may be banished from the Massachusetts Bay Colony. Please note that if that does occur, I will continue to pray for thou and thine family. Thou is such an inspiration to women everywhere. Thank thou for being a strong woman.

Sincerely,

ANONYMOUS FAN

WRITING LETTERS OF LOVE

Girl, you are as pretty as a hippopotamus playing in the water!

Okay, so maybe that particular sentiment won't get you too far, but you get the idea. Choose a historical figure, geographic location, event, or inanimate historical object and write a letter full of love. It can be from you, from another historical figure, from a historical event, or from an inanimate object. Use the blanks provided to pen some ideas you have before you write your final project.

STEPS TO TAKE:

1. Choose a historical figure, geographic location, event, or inanimate historical object that needs a lovey-dovey letter.

Ideas for who needs a love letter:

2. Investigate why a love letter is due to this person/event/thing. Why might someone be in love with person/event/thing? Write down any background information you find. You will want to use facts in your letter.

Background information:

3. Decide the motivation for writing the letter of love. Is the person seeking forgiveness, trying to get married to inherit a kingdom, just plain smitten, or wanting to meet for coffee?

What is the motivation?

4. In friendly letter format, write a letter of love from the viewpoint of the historical figure. You might seal your letter with a kiss!

Love Letter from a Chocolate Fan
to the Ancient Mayans

Dear Ancient Mayans,

I love you! I love, love, love you and all your chocolatey goodness.

Hershey Bars, Twix, chocolate pies, Mocha lattes, chocolate pudding, chocolate-covered raisins…why, none of those delectable goodies would be in existence if it were not for your discovery of the cacao plant! It is a royal delight! So royal that you served it to your royal Mayans.

I read that you enjoyed the cacao plant for its bitter tasting attribute, and that your version of chocolate was a spicy drink. I personally think cacao is better mixed with sugar. Lots of sugar to be exact, but I suppose you didn't know about that concoction.

Oh, Mayans, I am so thankful that you took the seed from the rainforest and began cultivating it for yourselves. I truly believe that cacao is the most important natural resource the world has to offer. After all, it is the main ingredient in chocolate!

Mayans, I especially love that you didn't keep the cacao plant a secret; secrets can be lost, and I would have hated if the secret of chocolate had disappeared with the death of your culture. Instead, you traded the cacao with the Aztecs.

It must have been hard to trade such a delicious commodity. Soon many tribes and civilizations were using cacao as currency, which was smart!

Why, nothing is more valuable than chocolate. I mean nothing!

Sometimes my sister gives me chocolate, and I do her chores. Sometimes, she gives me chocolate, and I do her homework. Let's keep that a secret though, okay?

I'm really sorry that the Spaniards came into your lands and did a bit (well, a lot) of damage. I can't wish that it had never occurred though, because they spread the love of chocolate around the world. Those stealthy Spaniards shipped cacao back to their homes and managed to keep the cacao a secret from the rest of Europe for over one hundred years! Well, I guess I can't really fault them. I sometime keep my chocolate bars secret from my mom.

Although if I kept my candy bars under my bed for one hundred years, I think they would be pretty disgusting.

Thankfully, the Spaniards figured out that mixing sugar, spices, and everything nice turned the cacao from bitter to chocolaty sweet goodness. Yummy!

The rest is history! A love affair of chocolate began once the rest of the world got hold of the sweet treat. Just think, it was you, dear Mayans, who first discovered the best taste my taste buds have ever met. I just adore you. I think I'm in L-O-V-E!

Much love,

ANNIE, A CHOCOLATE LOVER

Love Letter from Abraham Lincoln to Mary Todd

1841

My darling dear Mary Todd,

If only I could see your beautiful starry eyes and touch your silken hair. Oh, if only I could hear you speak French to me again, my love. Mon amie.

Will you ever forgive me? I admit that I was wrong, Mary. I was exponentially wrong to break off our engagement. The only excuse I can offer is that I was scared. Scared out of my mind.

I was born in a log cabin and couldn't quite grasp the concept that someone as learned and elegant as you would truly be happy with my humble self. I feel so slight compared to your refined self. Would your father the banker even approve of our betrothal?

I know he thinks that I might never make anything of myself, but I promise you that I will try to make you proud.

I will take you dancing, I will take you to dinners, and I will treat you to trips to the theater if only you will once again be my love.

Please forgive me, my love. Please allow me once again to court you in hopes of marriage. Send me a lock of your hair and you will forever be mine.

Your one true love,
ABRAHAM LINCOLN

TEXTING THROUGH HISTORY

"Text me" has become the new "call me."

Texting affords people the opportunity to use language in non-formal way of communication. This format is a great opportunity for students to create fun mini-reports.

An Idea for Using Text Performances in the Classroom:

Texting Aloud: Invite two students to pretend to be reading and composing their text messages aloud. Have them act like they are typing their messages in the moment. Have them react to the motions and events they are mentioning.

WRITING TEXTS

"OMG, u heard what?!?!"

Imagine that historical figures could text. How might their text logs look? Choose a historical figure and an event that they could be texting about. Use the blanks provided to pen some ideas you might have before your write your final project.

STEPS TO TAKE:

1. Choose a historical figure and a specific event with which they were associated.

Ideas:

2. Find out all the information you can about the event. Who was involved in the event? Who might your chosen person be texting? What would the chatters be saying to each other? Is the chat humorous, serious, or are they engaged in a fight?

Background Information:

3. Create the text log of the correspondence. Go ahead and write like you text. Try to convey as much information as possible using as little words as you can.

P.S. You might have to create a crack the code page, too. The ancients may have had a different text language then we do now. J TTYL

Paul Revere's Text Log

Dr. Joseph Warren **(DJ)**
Paul Revere **(P)**
William Dawes **(DAWES)**

DJ: Hey we need to talk.

P: Up Doc?

DJ: Got a job 4 u 2nite. Get ur horse ready. U going 4 a night ride.

P: It's dark & I'm ready 4 bed. Pz...let's wait till tomorrow.

DJ: Lazy—Get out of bed! Brits r mving to Lxington & Concord. U must warn Hancock & Adams b4 they get arrested. Brits going to seize our weapons in Concord, too. They can't take our arsenal.

P: OMG! I'll leave Boston now. Am I only 1 going?

DJ: I'm sending Dawes on diff path so that if 1 of u gets caught the other can warn the boys. U def need 2b careful.

P: Ok. I'll ride fast as I can. R Brits coming by land or H2O?

DJ: H20—2 lanterns must go up at Old North Church to warn every1 of their path.

P: Will do! TTYS

P: Made it 1/2way. I'm warning ppl along the way that the regs are coming. Everyone getting ready for the attack. Where do I go in Lxington 2 find Hancock & Adams?

DJ: @ Hancock—Clarke House. Gud luk.

P: Just warned them. They r ready for battle. Hancock said they would send those Brits back across the Atlantic J

DJ: Yay! Now what u doing?

P: I just met up w Dawes & Prescott. We going 2 ride on 2 Concord to warn them that Brits want 2 seize weapons. We will get those weapons ready 4 them. LOL they won't know what they have coming. L8R

DAWES: Help! Revere captured. We got stopped by roadblock. Me and Prescott escaped. But Brits have Revere. I hear shots. Ridin twrds Concord to warn them. Doesn't look good L

DJ: What?!?!?!

Texting Log with Sitting Bull and General Custer

GENERAL CUSTER: On road trip with my peeps from the 7th Cavalry in the Black Hills. My fingers are crossed for gold!

SITTING BULL: Sir, you and your peeps are not welcome here. My many friends are here to convince you of this message. You are about to take a Whoopin' from team #Lakota Sioux #Northern Cheyenne and #Arapaho tribes.

GENERAL CUSTER: Where did all of these Native Americans come from? THIS IS A TRAP!!!!!!!

SITTING BULL: General Custer, you epic failed in this one! #History is laughing at you. It will be #YourLastStand!

GENERAL CUSTER: General Custer and his Peeps have lost signal.

SITTING BULL: That is a beautiful horse. I think that I will keep him as a souvenir of this fun time that I spent with General Custer. Thanks for the memories General Custer!

Jane Addams and President Benjamin Harrison Text Log

JANE ADDAMS: I just helped establish my Hull House in Chicago to help the working class people and recent immigrants. #Gotthebacksoflessfortunatepeople #givingahelpinghand.

PRESIDENT BENJAMIN HARRISON: This is a noble experiment Ms. Addams. Thank you for helping those that cannot help themselves.

JANE ADDAMS: Everyone is entitled to a high-quality education #Lookingoutforimmigrants #BuildingatightercommunityinCHITOWN.

PRESIDENT BENJAMIN HARRISON: A nation owes all children an outstanding education. My administration spent the Benjamins on our national education system. #NATIONALRESPONSIBILITYANDDEBT.

JANE ADDAMS: Education is the key to addressing the ills of our society especially poverty. #STAMPOUTPOVERTY.

PRESIDENT BENJAMIN HARRISON: You are correct that poverty is a national concern. Large businesses are creating problems for a large portion of the American public. #CorruptionwithBig Business #GildedAge.

JANE ADDAMS: The American society created through big businesses has made it impossible for many to chase their dreams. My Hull House is designed to give the downtrodden a chance to once again succeed in this country. #RestoringandExtendingtheAmericanDream!

Muckraking Text Log Between Upton Sinclair and Ida Tarbell

IDA TARBELL: I am creating a ruckus on my end #StandardOil is not one of my Twitter followers.

UPTON SINCLAIR: It just comes with being a good muckraker. The meatpacking industry does not like me. #TheJungle opened some eyes# Public policy to reform the meatpacking industry.

IDA TARBELL: It is our job to expose corruption by corporations and political machines #PublicWatchdog.

UPTON SINCLAIR: The problem with capitalism is that some people try to use their influence and wealth to manipulate our political process to their advantage #CronyCapitalists #Graft #GildedAge.

IDA TARBELL: The public needs to be informed with our journalism about the crooked actions of companies and businessmen. #AmericanpeoplewillnotstandforCorruption Did my cartoon octopus create a ruckus?

UPTON SINCLAIR: I hope President Roosevelt is genuine in his support against the excesses of corporations. #UsetheBigStickforthePublicGood #TrustbusterintheWhiteHouse?

IDA TARBELL: I think that Mr. Roosevelt has some Progressive traits. #BigStickDefendstheNationalParks.

UPTON SINCLAIR: The values of Progressivism will clean up the graft and excesses of capitalism over the last 20 years. #AmericaisanoScroogeZone.

Cold War Text Log Between
Joseph McCarthy and Harry Truman

JOE MCCARTHY: Our government is filled with Communists #CommiesUnderEveryRock
Going to Share My list of U.S. Government Commies.

HARRY TRUMAN: You are blowing smoke Tail-Gunner Joe #SenatorWannabe-DemagogueMcCarthy #MissingProofForYourArguments.

JOE MCCARTHY: Mr. President, your administration has been soft on Communism. #NotToughColdWarrior #WhatHappenedtoChina?
#HowdidtheSovietsGetTheAtomicBomb?

HARRY TRUMAN: Have you forgotten Senator, that it was my tough stance against Stalin that started the Cold War? #StalinisnotoneofmyFacebookFriends #Yourapproachisformediaattention #GrowUpTailGunnerJoe.

JOE MCCARTHY: The United States must be vigilant in her fight against the spread of Communism and deal with any subversives #StrongColdWarrior.

HARRY TRUMAN: This does not mean that you smear the reputation of innocent people and trample their rights and liberties #SenatorMcCarthyisonawitchhunt.

JOE MCCARTHY: Mr. President, you are too afraid to roll up your sleeves to do what is necessary to defend American democracy. #TruePatriot #CommiesnotwelcomeintheU.S.

HARRY TRUMAN: Your tactics are going to get you into trouble Senator McCarthy #HistoryisgoingtotalksmackaboutTail-GunnerJoe.

PRESS CONFERENCES

"Breaking News! Breaking News!"

Today it is not uncommon for leaders, heroes, and even villains to speak to the media in a press conference. Press conferences give information about specific events. Writing press conferences is a great exercise for students to summarize events and study point of view and bias.

Ideas for Using Press Conferences in the Classroom:

TV Time: Students in the classroom take to the podium to read their press conference for all to hear. As an extension, students can take questions from the audience and answer in role.

Choral Read: All students in the classroom read a press conference aloud. Everyone has fun and builds fluency. Discuss the point of view and whether bias could have influenced the words spoken.

Anticipatory Set: Perform press conferences at the beginning of a unit to build excitement and intrigue about the subject.

Vivid Viewpoints: After student performances compare and contrast various viewpoints that were presented.

WRITING PRESS CONFERENCES

"Testing, testing, 1, 2, 3."

Imagine that historical figures give press conferences. What might they say in their speeches? Choose a historical figure and an event in which they are associated. Use the blanks provided to pen some ideas you might have before you write your final project.

STEPS TO TAKE:

1. Choose a historical figure and a specific event with which they were associated.

Ideas:

2. Find out all the information you can about the event. Who was involved? What might your historical figure say about an event? Is the person purely giving information or also trying to persuade the audience to think a certain way.

Background Information:

3. Write the press conference.

Monroe Doctrine Press Conference

Good morning, ladies and gentlemen. This brief statement is to address some of the statements during my inaugural address that have sparked some serious discussions in this country and Europe. The United States will not tolerate European powers meddling in the affairs of our states or in any other part of the New World. This part of the world is not a resource to be used at the whim of European powers. European powers should make no mistake that the United States will not abide interference in our affairs or that of our neighbors, and we will take whatever action necessary to ensure that the sovereign nations of Europe respect our wishes.

In turn, it is the pledge of the United States to likewise not interfere in the affairs of Europe. We will not seek out opportunities to meddle in other folks' affairs for our benefit. The United States will serve as an example with our foreign policy for the rest of the world to imitate. This is the role of this great country in this world—to be an example of what can happen when democracy is given an opportunity to flourish.

Clara Lemlich Press Conference

The United States must change. We cannot scream with a loud voice about our democratic principles and values and remain quiet about the injustice that took the lives of over one hundred women in the fire at the Triangle Shirtwaist Factory. To solve a problem, it is important to identify its cause. The problem facing America today is very straightforward: the business owners' lust for profits is not taking into consideration the needs of their workers. Over one hundred women that are mothers, sisters, aunts, and friends died because the management of the Triangle Shirtwaist Factory was too cheap to spend for proper safety requirements. This is not acceptable in this land that is supposed to value the rights and liberties of her citizens. My voice will not be silent about this injustice.

Tomorrow, I will help lead a strike against the owners of the Triangle Shirtwaist Factory. Our goal is to awake the outrage of our fellow citizens to this injustice that strikes at the fabric of this great country. Our message is straightforward: women are not fodder to be used and discarded at the whim of factory owners. We want safety precautions to prevent this problem from occurring again and higher wages. Our strike will not end until justice is done.

Caesar Chavez Press Conference

This brief statement is to announce the formation of the National Farm Workers Association. The purpose of the National Farm Workers Association is to represent the interests of Latino farm workers that are being underpaid and undervalued. As the Freedom Rides proved last year, people sadly have to fight for their rights in a democracy. People in power in this country rarely address the grievances of their disadvantaged citizens. It takes public pressure and continued effort for political leaders to take action against those that fill their coffers with campaign donations.

I want to be clear that I am not advocating violence. My approach is similar to how Dr. King, and those like him, are struggling for African Americans' rights. There is no need for violence because we are right. We are right now, and history will always record that our cause is justified. I will speak up for every Latino farm worker that is seen as invisible in 1962. After all, a nation conceived with the concepts of liberty and freedom is judged at the end of the day based on how she handles the disadvantaged and downtrodden.

Franklin D. Roosevelt Press Conference

Good morning ladies and gentlemen. My victory over President Hoover is the dawning of a new day for this country. The country may have fell apart under the careful watch of a Republican engineer, but my administration will look to rebuild this country for every citizen. Unlike President Hoover, I am not afraid to be creative in my solutions to problems that have recently plagued this country. My solutions will be designed to help those hurt the most by the economic maladies we face.

My "First One Hundred Days" in office will be spent aggressively addressing our economic situation. Congress had better be ready to work because I intend to send its members a variety of policies to get us started on the road to recovery. My first action will be to stabilize the currency issues in this country. People should be able to trust that their money is protected by putting it in a bank. I do not expect to solve all of the issues facing this country in my "First One Hundred Days." It will take the concerted effort of Congress working in conjunction with my administration and the work ethic and strength of citizens in this country to overcome our shared problems.

From my travels around this country, I believe that our citizens are up to the challenges that we face. The strength, character, and determination of the American people when applied can solve any problem.

John Ross Press Conference

The decisions from the Supreme Court in the cases of Cherokee Nation v. Georgia *and* Worcester v. Georgia *have restored my faith in the laws in this country. A country must be governed by laws not the passions of men. President Jackson, and men like him in Congress, have repeatedly tried to ship tribes from their lands in the Southeast. Their motivations are simply for their own avarice not for the benefit of my people. I will not rest on my laurels with these victories. I will continue to petition the elected representatives in Washington to pass legislation that respects and protects the rights and liberties of my people in this country.*

SCANDALS

"Did you hear about...?"

Gossip is the nature of the "social studies *scandal*." A scandal is a form of writing that students can read aloud, react to, and write themselves as a form of reporting as they capture the essence of a particular point of view of an individual, place, or thing. Add in a little humor or interest and you've got a winning piece of writing.

Ideas for Using Whines in the Classroom:

Scandal Report: Students in the classroom read their written scandals aloud for all to hear. Pretend that they are being read on a gossipy television talk show.

Choral Read: All students in the classroom read a scandal aloud together. Everyone has fun and builds fluency while acting out the scandal. Discuss why the topic is scandalous at that particular point in history.

Anticipatory Set: Perform a scandal at the beginning of a unit to build excitement about the subject. For example, start a unit about the 19th Amendment with a scandal about Seneca Falls.

Quick Assessment: Call on a student at the end of a lesson to create an ad-lib scandal. See if the student includes main content points.

Vivid Viewpoints: Discuss with students the different viewpoints of the scandals. Who might consider the information scandalous?

WRITING SCANDALS

Oh my goodness!

Choose a historical figure, geographical location, event, or inanimate historical object and write a scandal about the topic. Use the blanks provided to pen some ideas you have before you write your final project.

STEPS TO TAKE:

1. Choose a historical figure, geographic location, event, or inanimate historical object (i.e. building, artifact, or monument).

Topic ideas:

2. Search for facts about the topic and imagine why some of the facts might be scandalous at that time in history.

A few facts to include:

3. Here is the scoop—use the above facts to creatively write a few paragraphs that report the scandals. Write as if you are a news reporter, gossip columnist, or talk show host telling all the scandalous news. Use words they might utter and be persuasively whiney.

Scandal:

The Scandalous Life of Andrew Carnegie

The latest target of gossips around the country is none other than Andrew Carnegie.

Did you know that he wasn't even born in America? Well, he wasn't. Carnegie is from a country where they don't speak proper English – Scotland. His boyhood heroes were rebels most Americans have never even heard of – William Wallace, Robert Bruce, and Rob Roy.

Carnegie started out as a bobbin boy in a cotton factory. For the next fifteen years, he moved from one job to another. He worked as telegraph operator, on railroads, in the munitions business, you name it. The man had no stability. He didn't even go to school. Can you believe it? He was self-educated! He taught himself by constantly borrowing books.

Carnegie didn't even marry until he was in his fifties. When he did wed, it was to a woman more than twenty years younger than he.

He got into the steel around the same time he got hitched. He must have been crooked because he made a bunch of money. When he sold out in 1901 Carnegie had about 4% of all the wealth in the U.S.A.

Do you know what he did with all of that money? That foolish man practically gave it all away. How scandalous! He founded over 3,000 public libraries. What a foolish thing to do. People don't need free books to borrow! He built music halls for concerts. People don't need music! Carnegie even established pension funds so former employees could retire and not work. People don't need to retire! The man single handedly made it acceptable to be lazy in America.

By the time he died in 1919 Carnegie had give away over 350 million dollars. Could he possible have been more wasteful?

The Scandalous Life of Juan Ponce de Leon

The English know deep in their hearts that all Spaniards are crazy, mad, and cuckoo! If you don't believe that – here is the case of Juan Ponce de Leon.

Leon called himself an explorer and a conquistador. But what he really was – was a crazy old man. In his twenties, Ponce came to the New World to make his name and fortune and do great things for Spain.

He led a pretty normal life for a while. He married an innkeeper's daughter and had a family.

But then Ponce began to go crackers. He started feeling his age. He wanted to be young again. Some might say that a mid-life crisis is pretty normal for a guy in his forties. That may be true – but Ponce went nuts.

He fell for a ponzi scheme. Some natives fed the poor old boy a local legend about a fountain in Florida. This fountain supposedly would make a man young again. Could any idea be crazier?

Ponce fell for it hook, line, and sinker. He made not one but two voyages to Florida! The second voyage he made so he could colonize the place. Isn't that the wackiest thing you've ever heard? Two times he visited the Sunshine State, but he made not one single visit to the beach or Disney World.

Poor, poor Ponce, he never did find the fountain. But he did discover that the natives could make some pretty good slow-acting arrow poison from the sap of the Manchinee tree. The poor sap died from the tree sap. What a scandalous tale!

The Scandal of Seneca Falls

Another American Revolution stalks this great country. Unlike the first Revolution, this one does not seek freedom but privilege.

On July 19th and 20th, 1848, a secret convocation, consisting mostly of women, gathered in Seneca Falls, New York. An extremist religious group called Quakers purportedly organized the conference. While their husbands, brothers, and fathers innocently slept, radicals plotted to bring women to power in the United States.

Though most of the attendees kept their identity secret, outspoken troublemakers such as Frederick Douglass and Lucretia Mott spun their revolutionary rhetoric of disruption by openly advocating for women's rights.

In an act seeping of scandal, these people actually advocated for women having the right to vote. In a fiery Declaration of Sentiments, these women declared that "he" – meaning men, of course – "had never permitted "her" to exercise her inalienable right to the elective franchise."

The "Declaration" accused men of repeated "injuries and usurpations" toward women.

Now I know that most of you God fearing, righteous men are not aware of the so-called Seneca Falls Convention. But I warn you to be afraid. Act now to stop this evil movement. Also, be on the lookout. There may be one or more rebellious, power-seeking women sleeping in your own house.

The Scandalous Life of Eleanor Roosevelt

Eleanor Roosevelt may be the wife of the only President in American history to be elected four times. But sources close to the family reveal that scandal surrounds the former First Lady.

Her father notoriously yielded to the pressure of his own sadness and was largely an absentee from her life.

Eleanor is even friends with a known aviatrix and has even been known to go flying with this wild living adventuress, risking her very life. If she wanted a proper flying mate she should have sought out a male flyer such as the beloved Colonel Charles Lindbergh.

Mrs. Roosevelt has also been known to expose her dignity and the honor of her office by corresponding with children. She has actually written return letters to children! How immature.

The First Lady is also reportedly contemplating writing her own autobiography, doubtlessly aggrandizing her part in the great accomplishments of her husband. The proposed title tells it all – "My Story."

Shamelessly, when asked by *Good Housekeeping* to define the role of a modern wife's job, she replied that a wife needed to "develop her own interests, to carry on a stimulating life of her own ..." Can you believe that attitude?

At one point after FDR's first inauguration, Eleanor reportedly wrote to a friend that she contemplated divorcing the President, saying that her role as First Lady would curtail her own activities.

And then, of course, there is Mrs. Roosevelt's wardrobe. Her sense of style simply makes Mary Todd Lincoln look like a fashion plate. The woman wears $10 dresses! What a fashion scandal. She has no sense of propriety and even drives her own car.

Indeed, this is a dangerous woman to have so close to the head of the American government.

RUBRICS FOR ASSESSMENT

Rubrics are helpful tools for both teachers and students. They help teachers assess student work and provide students a list of expectations.

Provided are two sample rubrics you can use for the writing and performance pieces. It is recommended that you create a rubric that includes more specific expectations based upon the skills you desire your students to master. Here are some points to think about when constructing rubrics.

Your goal is to create a student assessment that allows students to showcase what they have learned.

Don't include extraneous information in your rubric. For example, don't include a category for spelling if that is not a objective you want to assess.

Identify specific levels of quality when creating your scale.

Be specific and concise in the language of your rubric.

Assess for more than just "surface-level" understanding. Your assessment piece should include opportunities for students to showcase deeper understanding of the content.

Make certain that the rubric will give you insight into student learning, help you identify patterns for the whole class, and make instructional decisions regarding individual students.

Think about how you might have to modify the rubric for individual students.

Share your rubric with students before they begin working on the assessment piece. Students should always know what is expected of them; learning should not be a mystery!

Consider leaving a place for written feedback on the rubric or have an individual conference with students to discuss the rubric.

WRITING PROJECT RUBRIC

Title of Project: _____

Student Name: _____

	1	2	3
WRITING	Lacks clarity.	Communicates information well.	Clear, complete, and tightly constructed.
UNDERSTANDING OF TOPIC	The student writing illustrates that the student does not have an understanding of the topic.	The student writing illustrates that the student somewhat understands the topic.	The student writing illustrates that the student has a firm understanding of the topic.
NUMBER OF CREDIBLE SOURCES USED	One.	Two to Four.	Five or more.
INFORMATION INCLUDED ABOUT THE TOPIC	Little or no factual information.	Includes basic factual information.	Includes a variety of interesting facts beyond the basics.
BIBLIOGRAPHY	Some bibliographic information is included but not in the correct format.	Some bibliographic information is included, and the format is correct.	All necessary information is included and is in the correct format.
ORGANIZATION	Not well organized.	Includes logical organization.	Organization flows with clarity and adds to interest.

Total Points _____/18

Grade _____

Additional Comments:

DRAMATIC PRESENTATION RUBRIC

Title of Project: _____

Student Name: _____

	1	2	3
ORGANIZATION	Information is not presented in a logical sequence that the audience can follow.	Information is presented in a logical sequence that the audience can follow.	Information is presented in a logical and interesting sequence that the audience can follow.
UNDERSTANDING OF TOPIC	The student presentation illustrates that the student does not have an understanding of the topic.	The student presentation illustrates that the student somewhat understands the topic.	The student presentation illustrates that the student has a firm understanding of the topic.
DELIVERY	Student mumbles or speaks softly.	Student's voice is clear.	Student uses a clear voice and dramatically and appropriately acts in the performance.
INFORMATION INCLUDED ABOUT THE TOPIC	Little or no factual information.	Includes basic factual information.	Includes a variety of interesting facts beyond the basics.
ORGANIZATION	Presentation is not well organized.	Presentation includes logical organization.	Presentation flows with clarity and adds to interest.
CONTENT KNOWLEDGE	Student is uncomfortable with content knowledge and is uncomfortable answering questions.	Student demonstrates partial knowledge and answers questions.	Student demonstrates full knowledge and easily answers questions.

Total Points _____/18

Grade _____

Additional Comments:

ACADEMIC REFERENCES

Burstein, J. & Knotts, G. (2010). From disconnected to connected: Using the visual performing arts to enhance social studies content and concepts. *Social Studies and the Young Learner*, 23(1), 239-247.

Kornfeld, J., & Leyden, G. (2005). Acting out: Literature, drama, and connecting with history. *The Reading Teacher*, 59(3), 230–239.

National Commision on Writing. (2003). The neglected "R": The need for a writing revolution *College Entrance Examination Board* (Vol. 9): New York, NY.

Rosler, B. (2008). Process drama in one fifth-grade social studies class. *Social Studies*, 99(6), 265-272.

Turner, T. (2004). *Essentials of elementary social studies* (3rd ed.). Boston, MA: Pearson.

ABOUT THE AUTHORS

DR. SARAH PHILPOTT earned her PhD from the Department of Theory and Practice in Teacher Education at the University of Tennessee, Knoxville. A former elementary and middle school teacher, she has contributed to books such as *Contemporary Social Studies: An Essential Reader* and has been published in numerous journals such as *Social Studies and the Young Learner*. She lives on a farm in TN with her husband and three young children. Sarah blogs at allamericanmom.net and is currently under contract to write a devotional for women who have experienced pregnancy loss.

DR. THOMAS N. TURNER is a Professor Emeritus of Social Science Education at The University of Tennessee, Knoxville. He is the author of numerous books, including *Essentials of Elementary Social Studies* and has authored over a hundred book chapters and journal articles. His research interests include drama in the classroom and children's literature.

DR. JEREMIAH CLABOUGH is an Assistant Professor of Social Science Education in the Department of Curriculum and Instruction at the University of Alabama at Birmingham. A former middle school teacher, he is one of the editors for *Getting at the Core of the Common Core with Social Studies* and lead author for *Unpuzzling History with Primary Sources*. His research interests include integrating primary sources, graphic novels, and trade books into the social studies classroom.

www.ingramcontent.com/pod-product-compliance
Lightning Source LLC
LaVergne TN
LVHW081346060426
835508LV00017B/1448